REPAST

REPAST
THE STORY OF FOOD

JENNY LINFORD

Thames & Hudson The British Museum

Contents

Introduction 7
Hunting 13
Gathering 29
Fishing 45
Agriculture: plants 63
Agriculture: animals 85
Travel and trade 107
Religion 123
Feasts 137

Alcohol 153

Preserving and processing 173

Cooking 195

Eating in 215

Eating out 233

Food and our future 248

Bibliography 250
Acknowledgments 252
Picture credits 252
Index 253

Introduction

Food is universal, yet particular. The need to eat is a biological imperative, one that omnivorous humans have responded to with much ingenuity over many millennia. While the requirement to eat is common to all of us, what we eat and how we eat it varies according to geography, climate, history and societal norms.

The need for food has helped to shape who we are as a species. Finding and sharing food influenced socializing and bonding within groups of hominins, our early ancestors, who eked out an existence scavenging scraps of meat from animal carcasses. Successful foraging and reliably obtaining nutrition through the making and use of tools – evidence of which dates from about two million years ago – also fed the calorie-hungry brain, supporting its development. The ability to make and use fire for cooking, which possibly began just over a million years ago in parts of Africa, assisted and accentuated the importance of meat in the early human diet, as well as the social bonding and cultural significance associated with sharing a meal by the fire.

For most of early human history, people lived as hunter-gatherers, finding their food in the wild; indeed, some still do, living in remote regions where this practice is best suited to their environment. However, after about 12,000 years ago, a gradual shift towards agriculture took place independently across the world. Rather than foraging and hunting, humans began relying for sustenance predominantly on the food they produced themselves through growing crops and rearing animals. With the need to tend crops and livestock came a settled rather than nomadic existence. The food surpluses created by farming as opposed to foraging saw human populations increase and people live together in larger, permanent communities.

Today, nearly half of the world's habitable land mass is given over to agriculture. Ensuring that people have enough food to eat is not a simple matter. The availability of food is affected by a range of factors, including adverse weather conditions, pests and diseases, and wars. We live in a world where malnutrition and famines still occur, as they have done throughout human history. At the other end of the spectrum, obesity has become a major and urgent health issue around the world. Responsible for millions of premature deaths each year, it affects not just wealthy countries but low- and middle-income ones as well.

Drawing on the British Museum's extensive collection, this book offers a special and distinct version of the story of food. All the images and objects that have been used to illustrate this story come from the British Museum and have been selected with the help of its expert curators.

Reindeer were an important source of food and materials during the last Ice Age in Europe. This drawing, engraved on a now damaged piece of bone, is about 14,000 years old, and depicts a young animal with a diagonal line through its shoulder, perhaps representing a spear. The drawing originally showed two reindeer, one slightly behind the other.

Drawing of reindeer on bone. 14,000 years old. La Madeleine, Tursac, France. Bone. H. 3.3 cm, W. 7.1 cm, D. 2 cm. Palart.419. Christy Collection.

Rather than focusing simply on food at the table in its final form, ready for consumption, *Repast* looks at food from a more fundamental perspective, exploring how humans have fed themselves through the ages. The book takes the reader on a journey from the hunting, gathering and fishing of wild foods – plant and animal – through the rise of agriculture, to the way we enjoy eating food with other people both in the home and outside it. As this book shows, as well as being essential to life, food is rich in social, cultural and religious associations.

Food has connective powers. The sharing of food is a basic act of hospitality, requiring trust on behalf of both the host and the guest. In our personal lives, food evokes memories; we associate particular foods and drinks with when and where we first encountered them, reminding us of our childhood or a special holiday. The sheer relatability of cooking and eating – activities we can all know and understand – makes the past seem closer. This is one reason, for example, why in recent decades so many stately homes have opened up their kitchens and kitchen gardens. As one studies the artefacts in this book, there is a jolt of recognition at seeing the familiar: a fish hook dating back to the

Below: In wealthy households, food was once served on sets of decorative, painted wooden plates called trenchers. This example is part of a set of twelve used for the dessert course. Trenchers sometimes featured mottoes to entertain or spark a conversation. The motto here reads: 'Men fhould beware & take great hede / To haffard frends wt ont great need / For a bird in hand is better far: / Than thre yt in the hedges are.'

Trencher plate, *c.* 1600. UK. Painted and gilded wood. Diam. 13.6 cm. 1896,0807.8.k. Donated by Sir Augustus Wollaston Franks.

Opposite: This drawing, attributed to the Bangladeshi artist Zainul Abedin, shows a family struck by the Bengal Famine of 1943. It may have been an early sketch for Ela Sen's book *Darkening Days*, published in 1944. Banned by the British authorities, the book chronicles the slow death by starvation of millions of Bengali peasants during the Second World War.

Attributed to Zainul Abedin, drawing of family during the Bengal Famine, 1943. Bangladesh. Chinese ink on paper. H. 45 cm, W. 29 cm. 2012,3027.1. Purchase funded by the Modern Museum Fund.

late Ice Age; a long, slender drinking straw made in Ur around 2600 BCE; a shopping list written in Latin on a wooden tablet in the Roman fort of Vindolanda in northeast England between the late first and early second centuries CE. The writer of this list – perhaps responsible for stocking the fort's mess, judging by the quantities involved – instructs the shopper to buy 'a hundred apples, if you can find nice ones, a hundred or two hundred eggs, if they are for sale … at a fair price'. The list-writer's concerns over the quality of ingredients and being overcharged are shared by food shoppers to this day.

In an age of social media and mobile phones, we are bombarded with glossy images of appetizing dishes: mouth-watering cakes, tempting bowls of pasta, succulent steaks. The objects and images in *Repast* offer a far more varied take on food. They are diverse and intriguing, selected across time and place: an Egyptian model of a group of brewers dating back to around 2050–2000 BCE, a dainty nineteenth-century Japanese netsuke carved in the form of a tea bowl and whisk, a Tiepolo drawing of a Venetian cafe scene. When one looks through *Repast*, the long-standing human fascination with food is clear.

Above: Vietnamese artist Nguyen Cong Do painted this image during the Vietnam War for a poster intended to drum up support for the war effort. The striking image of tanks being transformed into tractors is a piece of propaganda – its message being that, if we fight now, not only will we be able to resume farming, but we will farm in a modern way.

Nguyen Cong Do, painting, 1972. Vietnam. Gouache on paper. H. 54.5 cm, W. 79 cm. 1998,1215,0.2. Donated by the British Museum Friends and the British Museum Society.

Opposite: Special wooden dishes, such as this one carved in the form of a human figure, were used by Fijian priests in *burau* drinking rites. The dish would be filled with a peppery, narcotic drink called *yagona* (known as *kava* in other Pacific regions), which would be drunk undiluted by the priest through a straw, enabling them to commune with the spirits of their ancestors.

Bowl, early 19th century. Fiji. Wood. H. 26.7 cm, W. 14 cm. Oc1842,1210.127. Donated by Sir Edward Belcher.

Hunting

For millennia, one of the principal means by which humans provided sustenance for themselves was hunting. Archaeological remains from the Olorgesailie region in Kenya suggest that early humans ambushed, caught and butchered large animals around 1 million years ago; scavenging for the carcasses of animals killed by other predators was another, ancient way of sourcing meat. By around 50,000–100,000 years ago, hunting was a key human activity. The meat derived from hunting was a valuable source of energy and protein; in fact, evidence indicates that hunting, together with food gathering, provided a diet rich in nutritious foods.

In hunter-gatherer societies, the meat obtained through hunting was shared among the group, especially when it was large game. Geography affected both the type and the quantity of prey available to hunter-gatherers. In the circumpolar regions, for example, potential prey included such large sea mammals as walruses and seals. In Europe 13,000 years ago, reindeer were plentiful, providing the humans who hunted them with not only meat but also skin, bones and antlers to use for clothing and tools. Similarly, the wild bison that lived on the plains of North America sustained Native Americans for thousands of years. Even after the arrival of agriculture, hunting continued alongside the rearing of livestock, with wild game a key part of the human diet.

Humans have developed a variety of techniques and equipment for hunting their prey. Game drives, in which animals are herded into confined or dangerous places like pits or bogs in order to trap them, were used from at least 115,000 years ago. Among the equipment used for hunting were snares, decoys, lures, nets and hides. Animals were used as well. Dogs, among the first animals to be domesticated, were taken on hunts both to help tackle such dangerous beasts as wild boar and to retrieve wounded or dead animals. Birds of prey were trained to use their natural abilities as winged hunters for the benefit of humans. Riding on horses allowed hunters to chase swift-moving prey, including deer. Weapons in the hunter's arsenal historically included spears, boomerangs and other kinds of throwing stick, bows and arrows, blowpipes with poisoned darts, and clubs. As firearms developed during the Middle Ages, hunters began using guns – weapons that are widely used in hunting today.

While hunting was originally carried out for the purpose of providing food and clothing, it later became a sport in its own right – possibly in ancient Egypt, but perhaps even earlier. Regardless of its exact origins, hunting for sport continues to be a recreational activity enjoyed by social elites, including royalty and aristocracy, with animals hunted for the thrill of the chase rather than in order to put food on the table.

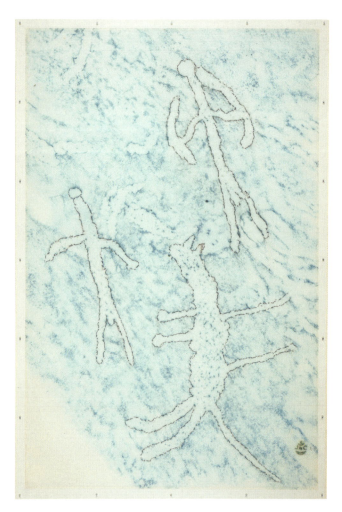

Above: During the last Ice Age, about 14,000 years ago, mammoths were the largest land animals. Their size and strength perhaps inspired this sculpted image made from reindeer antler, which formed part of a spear-thrower – the handle of which is now missing. Originally, the tail curled up as a hook for the base of the spear, enabling the hunter to throw it further and harder and bring down such prey as bison, horse and reindeer.

Spear-thrower, 14,000 years old. From Montastruc, France. Reindeer antler. L. 12.4 cm, W. 6 cm, D. 1.5 cm. Palart.551. Christy Collection.

Left: This rubbing, from an ancient piece of rock art, depicts Indigenous Australians hunting kangaroo. One of the human figures appears to be holding a boomerang. Before being cooked, kangaroos were put on a fire to singe off their hair; they were then placed in a hole and covered with charcoal and hot stones.

Rubbing, made by C. W. Cutten, J. G. Cutten, M. W. Philpott and J. C. Philpott, 1968–1973. Sturt's Meadows, Australia. Paper. H. 91.5 cm, W. 60.9 cm. Oc1974,07.29.

Caribou are an important animal for the Innu, both spiritually and as a source of food, clothing and shelter. Garments, skilfully made from hides, are warm, water-repellent and durable. This striking hunting coat is decorated with patterns that depict visions of caribou migration routes for a particular winter season, providing the person wearing it with power and guidance.

Coat, 1830–1853. Likely Innu, Northeastern Canada. Caribou skin. H. 115 cm, W. 75 cm. Am1991,11.1.

INUIT HUNTING

The Arctic region is home to 4 million people. Of these, 10 per cent are Indigenous, belonging to one or more of forty different cultural groups, including the Aleut and Inuit of Alaska, Canada and Greenland. Living in the frozen Arctic, where food resources are limited, presents a series of challenges for these communities. Hunting remains central to the Inuit way of life, with animals providing a vital source of both food and warm clothing.

For centuries, there has been a seasonal pattern to hunting in the Arctic region, although this is being affected by climate change. In early spring, migrating sea mammals return to northern waters, congregating where the open water meets the frozen shoreline. As spring continues and the days lengthen, sunlight generates an abundance of algae in the water – the foundation of a marine food chain for such sea mammals as seals, which are an important food source for Inuit. On the land, caribou is the main game animal, hunted primarily in the autumn, while birds are also hunted and eaten.

In this harsh, unforgiving environment, a deep understanding of the fauna and of weather conditions is essential to successful hunting. The skills and knowledge needed for hunting are passed down from generation to generation. Before they began using guns, Inuit hunters used their knowledge of Arctic animals to get close to them. They stayed upwind of their prey and disguised themselves – for example, by wearing wooden helmets in the shape of a seal's head. They also mimicked animal behaviour, using 'scratchers' made from wood and seal claws to scratch the ice as they approached and produce a sound familiar to the seals.

In traditional Inuit animism, the hunting of animals is seen as the giving and receiving of gifts. Hunters show respect for the animals they hunt in a variety of ways: making their hunting weapons with great care, sharing food, and treating the animals' remains with reverence. It is also believed that, by wearing parts of an animal, including sealskin and caribou hide, the hunter attains the qualities and abilities of that animal.

Inuit have hunted bowhead whales using various forms of toggle harpoon for a thousand years. *Umiaqs* – large, skin-covered, wooden-framed open boats that can hold up to twenty people yet are light enough to transport on sledges – were traditionally used for whaling and for hunting walruses. They are still used for hunting trips today, alongside more modern, motor-powered boats. Harpoons were also used by solo hunters in kayaks to catch seals and sea otters.

Butchering and storing the catch are the next stages of the hunting process. Meat and fish are preserved by drying, salting or freezing before being stored in ice cellars, dug into the permafrost. This vital food resource is then used to support the Inuit through lean times.

Above: Whales have been hunted by Inuit for many years. As with other Inuit hunting tools, whaling equipment is carefully made in order to show respect for the animals. Inuit use harpoons to catch whales; this whale-shaped box was used to store stone harpoon points.

Box, before 1855. Collected from Kotzebue Sound, Alaska, USA, likely made by Iñupiat carver. Wood, hemp. H. 9.5 cm, W. 10 cm, D. 33.5 cm. Am1855,1126.64.a-b. Donated by John Barrow.

Opposite: Seal hunting continues to be an important part of the Inuit way of life. A number of seal species are hunted. The seals provide not only an important source of food, but also materials for clothing and shelter.

Lucassie Tookalook, 1985. Printed in Puvirnituq, Canada. Stone-cut print in green ink on paper. H. 50 cm, W. 69 cm. 2012,2014.10.

Below: Ovid's *Metamorphoses* includes the myth of the Calydonian Boar. Diana, goddess of hunting, sends a ferocious giant boar to ravage the kingdom of Calydon because its ruler, King Oeneus, has insulted her. A party of brave hunters, including Meleager, the king's son, and Atalanta, succeed in killing the monster.

Plate, painted by Orazio Fontana, 1544. Urbino, Italy. Earthenware. Diam. 24.1 cm. 1855,1201.75.

Opposite, top: In the ancient world, the wild boar was regarded as formidable prey. Hunting the powerful animal required courage and skill; legendary heroes Odysseus and Hercules hunted boars. This Corinthian krater, a vessel used for diluting wine with water, shows a huge boar being hunted by spear-wielding men and their dogs.

Krater, *c.* 575–550 BCE. Made in Corinth, Greece, excavated near Capua, Italy. Pottery. H. 30.9 cm, Diam. 27.6 cm. 1772,0320.6.+.

Below: This woodblock print depicts a famous Japanese hunting scene. In 1193, shogun Minamoto no Yoritomo hosted a hunting party at the foot of Mount Fuji. A huge wild boar charged at him but was killed by one of his brave companions, the warrior Nitta Shiro Tadatsune.

Kitao Masayoshi (Kuwagata Keisai), the hunting of a boar near Mount Fuji, late 1780s. Japan. Colour woodblock diptych print on paper. H. 33.5 cm, W. 48.2 cm. 1949,1112,0.2.1-2.

Above: This fragment of a tomb-painting represents Nebamun, an ancient Egyptian who was buried in the city of Thebes around 1350 BCE. He is shown fowling in the marshes, holding a throw-stick in one hand and clasping three egrets in the other. A cat is depicted catching three of the birds startled by the hunt.

Tomb-painting, 18th Dynasty, c. 1350 BCE. Thebes, Egypt. Painted plaster. H. 98 cm, W. 115 cm, D. 22 cm. EA 37977.

Opposite, top: As the use of guns for killing birds became more widespread, the guns themselves evolved, becoming lighter and easier to handle. Shooting overhead at birds on the wing was regarded as testing the skill of the hunter. Dogs were trained to retrieve the fallen birds.

Thomas Bewick, from *History of British Birds*, c. 1791–1804. UK. Wood engraving on paper. H. 4.4 cm, W. 8.1 cm. 1882,0311.3550. Donated by Isabella Bewick.

Opposite, bottom: Titled *Zuogh dal cacciator* (Game of the Hunter), this 1699 Italian game board depicts a number of ways in which birds were hunted at the time. As well as being shot at with guns and bows and arrows, they were caught with the use of lures, nets and hides.

Giuseppe Maria Mitelli, *Zuogh dal cacciator* (Game of the Hunter), 1699. Italy. Etching on paper. H. 25.2 cm, W. 43.2 cm. 1852,0612.462.+.

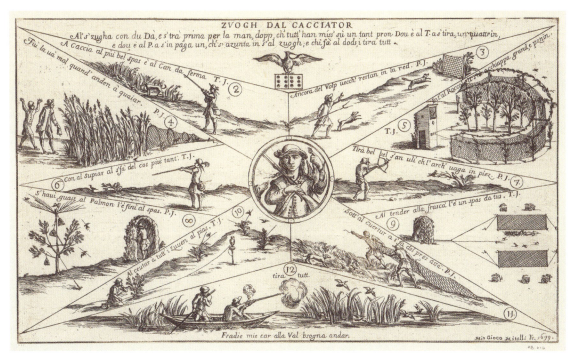

GAME

'Game' is traditionally used to describe the meat of wild animals and birds that have been hunted by humans for food or sport. Exactly which species constitute game birds or game animals varies from country to country, reflecting the local environment and the fauna found there. Wild animals classified as game range from rabbits and hares to antelope and elk; the species of bird considered game include pigeon, quail, snipe and wild turkey. The idea of game being 'wild' is itself also shifting; in some countries, game birds or animals, including deer, are reared in protected environments in order to ensure a supply for sport. In rural communities, hunting for game is still a popular and important way of supplementing diets.

Increasingly, the hunting of game has become subject to legal controls, as laws protecting endangered wild creatures have been brought in. The hunting of certain species is now banned. In France, for example, it is now illegal to hunt such songbirds as ortolans, which were a highly prized delicacy. Many countries in Europe have strictly prescribed game seasons, which prohibit hunting during the breeding season to protect the populations of game animals and birds while they breed and rear their young.

This ceramic vessel, a product of the Moche civilization of northern Peru, depicts a deer hunt. On top of the vessel is the sculpture of a young deer, while the painted scene features a ritual deer hunt, in which the animal is pursued on foot by a warrior dressed in regalia and accompanied by a hound.

Vessel, 100–800 CE. Trujillo, Peru. Pottery. H. 23.7 cm, W. 14.8 cm, D. 20.4 cm. Am1909,1218.65. Donated by Henry Van den Bergh through Art Fund (as NACF).

For centuries, fast-running hares were hunted with swift, agile greyhounds. Coursing with dogs, including greyhounds and lurchers – where the prey is found by sight, not by scent, and chased over a long distance – was a popular hunting technique in Europe during the Middle Ages and early modern period.

Adriaen van de Venne, a huntsman with his greyhound, *c.* 1620–26. The Netherlands. H. 9.6 cm, W. 15.3 cm. 1978,0624.42.23. Donated by HM Government.

From a culinary perspective, the flesh of game animals – which live active lives and eat a varied diet – is valued for its depth of flavour, often described as 'gamey'. Because the lives of these animals are filled with movement, their flesh can also be lean and tough. This led to the practice of hanging game meat in a cool place for a period of time to mature it, making the meat more tender and the gamey flavour more pronounced. Certain culinary techniques are characteristic of game cookery. Marinades for game are often made from acidic ingredients like wine or yoghurt, plus herbs and spices for flavour, which help to tenderize it. Lean meat is usually cooked rare, so as not to make it tough. Conversely, the long, gentle cooking in such braised dishes as curries, pasta sauces and stews is also effective. Larding cuts of game with pieces of fat, wrapping it in protective rashers of bacon or spreading it generously with butter before cooking are other ways of ensuring succulence. Classic European accompaniments to game are often fruit-based; one finds elk with lingonberry jam or sauce in Sweden, while in Britain jellied preserves made from redcurrants or rowan berries are served with venison, grouse and partridge.

Historically, certain game animals acquired the status of delicacies, enjoyed by the social elite. In Imperial China, wild venison, pheasant, and deer tails and tendons were sent in tribute to the court by hunters in the northeast. To this day, game such as grouse, hare and kudu is served as a luxury on the menus of upmarket restaurants. With increased urbanization around the globe and the consequent loss of natural habitat and the fauna that lived among it, the meat of wild animals has become less widely consumed than in the past.

Historically, hunters used horns to signal to one another and their dogs, helping to keep humans and animals together. This twelfth-century elephant-ivory horn, decorated a century later with silver mounts depicting courtly scenes with hunting dogs, deer, hares and heraldry, reflects the high status of hunting in the medieval period.

Hunting horn, horn 12th century, enamelled silver bands 1325–50 CE, early 18th-century silver fittings near the mouthpiece. Savernake Forest, UK. Ivory, leather, silver, enamel. L. 63.5 cm. 1975,0401.1. Purchased with contribution from Art Fund (as NACF), Pilgrim Trust and Worshipful Company of Goldsmiths.

Boomerangs have come to symbolize Indigenous Australian culture. The earliest known example dates to about 10,000 years ago. They were used for a range of purposes, including the hunting of such birds and animals as emu, kangaroo and other marsupials. Boomerangs could also be used to kill fish that had become trapped in rock pools.

Boomerang, before 1955. Woomera Range, Australia. Wood. H. 62.2 cm, W. 23.1 cm, D. 1.4 cm. Oc1955,06.1. Donated by Mrs M. B. Follett.

Above: This quiver, used to carry blowpipe darts, is made from a section of bamboo with a basketry lid. Blowpipes were once used widely in Southeast Asian societies for hunting game at relatively close range in dense forests. Prized for being silent weapons, they could also be fired in rapid succession. Poison was sometimes added to the tips of the darts.

Quiver with woven basketry lid, 1850s–1900. Semai people, Perak, Malaysia. Bamboo, fibre, wood. H. 29 cm, Diam. 7 cm. As1910,-.167.a-b. Donated by Hugh Campbell, collected by Sir Archibald Campbell, 1st Baron Blythswood.

Right: The nomadic Hazda people of Tanzania live by hunting and gathering. Most of the meat eaten by Hazda people is obtained by solitary male hunters using a bow and arrow. Arrows with wooden points (*hik'o*) are used for hunting small game, including birds. Using a harpoon arrow helps reduce the chance of a wounded animal escaping the hunter.

Harpoon arrow, 20th century. Made by Hazda people, Tanzania. Wood, guinea fowl feather. H. 110 cm, W. 5 cm, D. 3.5 cm. Af1970,12.12.

Opposite: Falconry was a favourite sporting pursuit in the Mughal courts, enjoyed by nobles and royalty. It was also a popular theme in Mughal art. This seventeenth-century painting depicts Prince Daniyal, standing, with a bird of prey perched on his right hand, which is covered by a hawking glove.

Painting, late 16th century. Mughal school. Ink on paper, album leaf from *Hindu and Persian Miniatures and Penmanship*, an album containing 62 calligraphies and paintings. H. 29.7 cm, W. 18.7 cm. 1974,0617,0.10.10.

Right, top: Even when farming provided sufficient food, hunting with birds of prey was enjoyed as a skilful, high-status sport. This fourteenth-century elephant-ivory mirror case, a luxury item, shows a knight and his lady on horseback, their hawks perched attentively on their right hands.

Mirror case, 1325–75 CE. France. Ivory. H. 10.7 cm, D. 0.9 cm. 1856,0623.103.

Right, bottom: The falconer in this Chinese painting stands with his bird of prey perched on his forearm. His costume and facial features suggest that he is possibly a Khitan hunter. During their brief rule of China (915–1125), the nomadic Khitan further spread the practice of falconry across the region.

Painting, formerly attributed to Chen Juzhong, 13th century. China. Ink and colour on silk. H. 24.8 cm, W. 26.3 cm. 2010,3031.1. Purchased from Eskenazi Ltd, with contribution from Brooke Sewell Permanent Fund.

Gathering

Until the development of agriculture, gathering wild foods was an essential way for humans to provide sustenance for themselves, with gathered foods – mostly of the unprocessed plant variety – forming an important part of the diet. Foodstuffs that were gathered from the wild included plant-based items, such as leaves, roots, seeds, fruits, nuts and seaweeds, as well as molluscs, fungi, eggs, insects and honey from wild bees. As our hunter-gatherer ancestors migrated around the planet, they adapted to life in a variety of habitats, some living by the sea, others in tropical forests. Research suggests that the range of foodstuffs obtained through foraging, alongside those derived from hunting and fishing, resulted in a varied diet.

Hunter-gatherers – also known as foragers – lived in small groups, sharing the food they found or caught with each other. They had a mobile way of life, moving from place to place as the natural resources in their area became depleted. Their movements were also patterned by the changing seasons and the migration of birds, fish and animals. Depending on the natural resources available, each band of hunter-gatherers required sizeable areas of land on which to support itself; one estimate is that between 18 and 500 square kilometres were needed. A nomadic way of life meant that, for practical reasons, possessions were few and portable.

Hunter-gatherers had a deep understanding of the natural world around them, including the very necessary knowledge of which wild foods were safe to eat, which were dangerous, and which could be used for healing purposes. One important skill for gathering was the ability to create containers in which to place and carry gathered foodstuffs. Basket weaving is an ancient and widespread craft. Historically, a range of plant materials were used in the construction of baskets: tree bark, plant roots, leaves, sedge, grasses and kelp. Baskets were made in a variety of forms for different uses, from gathering tubers to carrying water.

With the rise of agriculture, hunter-gathering diminished as a way of life. Today, however, hunter-gatherer societies can still be found around the world, among them the San of Southern Africa, the Yanomami of Brazil and Venezuela, and the Sentinelese of the Andaman Islands. In industrialized nations, some knowledge of wild foods remains, with people still undertaking hunting and gathering, though often for recreational rather than survival purposes. Rural traditions of collecting wild fruit, edible flowers, nuts and fungi persist to this day, with the practice often passed down through the generations. Certain wild foods – powerfully scented truffles, such flavourful wild mushrooms as porcini or matsutake, sea urchins – have acquired a particular cachet, sought out as exclusive delicacies and served as expensive luxuries in upmarket restaurants.

For a Baka woman, a basket and a machete are essential tools, with basketry regarded as an important and valuable skill. There are essentially two types of Baka basket: the *gie*, a loose-weave carrying basket used for gathering edible plants and carrying possessions; and the *mbeka*, a close-weave basket generally used for storage.

Basket, 1970s. Made by Baka people, Cameroon. Rhizome or rattan (?). H. 26.5 cm, W. 26.5 cm, D. 26.5 cm. Af1979,15.31.

Rigid open baskets from the rainforest region of Queensland, Australia, are traditionally made by men. This example is documented as being used to collect Moreton Bay chestnuts. Such nuts are poisonous when fresh, but Aboriginal people have made use of them for thousands of years, carefully preparing the nuts by soaking them in running water.

Basket, before 1872. Made by Aboriginal Australians, Rockingham Bay, Australia. Cane, fibre. H. 48.5 cm, W. 49.5 cm, D. 35 cm. Oc,+.1185. Donated by John Ewen Davidson.

Left: Birch bark is an important resource for the Indigenous Peoples of North America, who prize the natural material for its versatility and water-resistant properties. Strips of bark, carefully cut from birch trees, are shaped into containers and held together with pieces of split root, as in the case of this berry basket.

Basket, late 20th century. Made by Dakelh, also known as Carrier, British Columbia, Canada. Root, birch bark, synthetic fibre. H. 24.6 cm, W. 28.5 cm, D. 28.5 cm. Am1988,13.8. Donated by Mrs Kythe Beaumont.

Below: In the Malaysian state of Sarawak, on Borneo, there is a long tradition of producing a range of baskets from local plant materials, each with a specific use. This small rigid basket with a head strap was for harvesting rice and collecting vegetables and fruit, whether cultivated in fields or growing wild in the countryside.

Basket, made by Agil, mid-20th century. Long Lungan, Borneo. Rattan, bamboo, leaf, iron. H. 27 cm, Diam. 28.5 cm. As1988,22.61.

Left: Among the food-gathering tools employed by the Indigenous Peoples of North America were digging sticks, made from durable hardwoods including Pacific yew. In work usually carried out by women, the strong, narrow sticks were used to dig out edible roots and tubers, as well as such shellfish as clams.

Digging stick, 19th century. Made by Kwakwaka'wakw, Northwest Coast Peoples, found at Xumtaspi, British Columbia, Canada. Yew. H. 82 cm, W. 6.5 cm, D. 4 cm. Am1958,02.8. Donated by Royal Botanic Gardens, Kew.

Right: Indigenous Australians have a deep knowledge of their country's fauna and flora. For thousands of years, they have been gathering nectar from the bush, appreciating the sweet flavour of this sugar-rich liquid. This hook was used to pull down the flowers of Banksia trees so that beads of nectar could be sucked from the blooms.

Hook, before 1839. Swan River, Australia. Wood, resin, fibre. H. 208.7 cm, W. 2.5 cm, D. 1.9 cm. Oc1839,0620.65. Donated by Samuel Neil Talbot.

Mangrove oysters are an important source of food in the West African country of Guinea-Bissau. Gathering them is physically arduous work, mainly carried out by women, with the risk of drowning in the mangrove swamps a real hazard. Made from iron and wood, this tool is used for knocking the firmly attached oysters off mangrove roots.

Tool, 1980s. Made by Nalu people, Guinea-Bissau. Iron, wood. H. 32.5 cm, W. 22.5 cm, D. 4 cm. Af1989,05.104.

WATER

Water – the inorganic compound H_2O – is vital to life on Earth. Up to 60 per cent of the adult human body, by weight, is made of water. To prevent dehydration and stay alive, we need to consume water, which is also found in food, on a daily basis. Water is needed not just for human consumption, but also for livestock and to irrigate crops; over the centuries, communities have constructed complex water-management systems, such as the *subak* in Bali, Indonesia, a cooperative irrigation system that uses canals and weirs to share water among the paddy fields. Ensuring access to fresh water has been important to societies throughout the ages and continues to be to this day. Historically, many human settlements were built near rivers; one sees this pattern in the world's great cities. Water is also important as a means for transporting goods for trade.

In addition to being fundamental to life, water plays a key role in the kitchen, where it is used for washing up and maintaining cleanliness. It is also widely used in cooking: it is the medium in which we boil foodstuffs like grains, pulses, vegetables and pasta to soften them and make them edible, while the power of heated water is used for steaming a range of foods, from fish to puddings. Water is employed as a heat-diffuser in a bain-marie, a piece of kitchen equipment used in the preparation of such delicately textured dishes as baked custards. In the form of ice, water is also important in the chilling of food and drink.

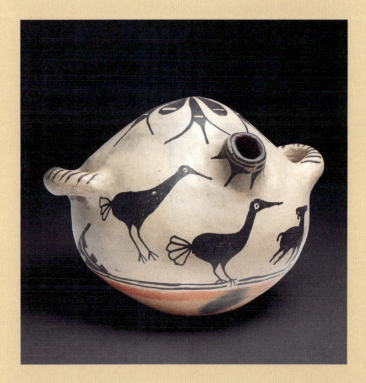

Water is a precious resource, especially to inhabitants of semi-arid regions. This water bottle is thought to have been made by Zuni people, of what is now northwest New Mexico, who have a long tradition of producing both ritual and functional pottery vessels – a tradition they continue to this day.

Water bottle, before 1888. Likely Zuni, New Mexico, USA. Pottery. H. 16 cm, W. 22.5 cm, D. 19 cm. Am1888,0517.13. Donated by John I. Covington.

The distinctive, fluid form of this traditional Malaysian water bottle is based on the shape of a gourd, hence its Malay name *labu air*, meaning 'water gourd'. It is made from locally produced earthenware, which, because it is porous, allows the water in the bottle to stay cool through the natural process of evaporation.

Water bottle, late 19th century. West Malaysia. Earthenware. H. 28.2 cm, Diam. 19.6 cm. As1905,0316.21. Donated by Leonard Wray.

Through the ages, people have endowed water with special associations and magical properties, including the ability to bestow fertility. Natural springs were thought to be home to spirits, such as water nymphs, and were worshipped in water cults; the notion of blessed or holy water is an ancient one. In some religions, immersion in water is regarded as purifying, as in the case of baptism in Christianity.

Many people have consumed water for its perceived health benefits. Mineral springs were valued for their health-giving qualities and used to treat certain ailments. Chalybeate, or iron-bearing waters, were drunk for anaemia, sulphurous waters were used for skin conditions, and saline water as a purgative. 'Medicinal' spa waters were bottled and sold; bottled mineral water remains a popular drink to this day.

Purity in potable water is a precious commodity. Historically, concerns over the quality of drinking water led people in towns and cities to turn to alternative beverages, including beer, which was regarded as safer. During the nineteenth century in Britain, a campaign to ensure public water supplies was supported by the Temperance movement. By the 1940s, the industrialized world had largely accepted that providing water to urban households was a public duty, and water networks were put in place.

Below: Edible seaweeds – part of the marine algae family – have been eaten in Britain since about 6000 BCE. In the nineteenth century, the fact that such seaweeds could be gathered freely on seashores made them an important source not only of food but also of work for low-income families.

Joseph Samuel Alpenny, *Gathering Sea Weed*, 1825. Published in London, UK. Lithograph on paper. H. 16.6 cm, W. 13 cm. 1861,1012.2303.

Opposite, top: Among the edible bivalves consumed by humans is the common mussel (*Mytilis edulis*). It lives on seashores, growing in dense clusters on rocks to which it attaches itself by threads known as byssus, and has long been harvested as a food source.

Adriaen van de Venne, a mussel-seller, *c.* 1620–26. The Netherlands. Drawing on paper. H. 9.6 cm, W. 15.2 cm. 1978,0624.42.84. Donated by HM Government.

Opposite, bottom: Seaweed has been eaten in Japan for many centuries. The Taiho code, an administrative and penal code issued in 701 CE, included seaweed among the marine products that were to be sent to the court as tax payment. This calm scene depicts two female seaweed gatherers, diligently at work.

Utagawa Kuniyoshi, *Ōmori*, 1830–35. Japan. Colour woodblock print on paper. H. 25.4 cm, W. 36.7 cm. 2008,3037.03601. Gift of Prof. Arthur R. Miller to the American Friends of the British Museum.

Below: An appreciation of wild and seasonal foods is at the heart of Japanese cuisine. Wild mushrooms are much enjoyed, with the rare matsutake mushroom – found in pine forests in autumn – valued for its aroma, flavour and texture, and regarded as a great delicacy.

Cho Gessho, old man and boy mushroom-gathering, 1814. Japan. Colour woodblock print on paper. H. 27.7 cm, W. 34.2 cm. OA+,0.196.

Opposite, top: Foraging for wild fungi has a long tradition in European countries and continues to this day. It is a practice that requires knowledge of which fungi are safe to eat, as many species are inedible and some toxic.

Peter De Wint, still-life with Chinese vase and basket of mushrooms, 1784–1849. UK. Drawing on paper. H. 21.3 cm, W. 29 cm. 1890,0512.61.

Opposite, bottom: There is the suggestion of rural plenty in this picture of a fen farm, from the herd of cows to the distant windmill. The woman's apron amply filled with freshly gathered field mushrooms adds to the sense of bounty.

Robert Walker Macbeth, *A Fen Farm*, 1890. Published in London, UK. Etching on paper. H. 38.2 cm, W. 74.5 cm. 1893,0718.36. Donated by Thomas Agnew & Sons.

L.D.S PETER DE WINT

HONEY

Human beings have an innate fondness for sweetness – one of the five basic taste types that the taste receptors on our tongues can identify. Long before sugar was first produced, honey was one of the world's great sweeteners. Honey is created by bees from concentrated nectar gathered from flowers and stored as a food to nourish bee colonies. In its lifetime, the average worker bee will produce one-tenth to one-twelfth of a teaspoon of honey.

Humans first gathered honey from the wild, tracking bees back to their nests in order to find their honey stores – a practice that continues to this day. Intriguingly, a shared interest in finding honey has seen people in parts of tropical Africa develop a partnership with the greater honeyguide bird (*Indicator indicator*). The bird leads large mammals, including people, to honey-bee nests, waits until the nests have been broken open and the honey eaten or harvested, and then eats what is left. Honey-hunting, as the collecting of honey from wild bees is known, is depicted in the ancient rock art of Southern Africa and Europe. In the Araña Caves near Bicorp in eastern Spain, a cave painting believed to be 8,000 years old shows a human figure collecting honey from a bees' nest while bees swarm around them.

Beekeeping, in which people care for bees in order to then harvest their honey and wax, can be traced back as far as the ancient Egyptians, with illustrations of hive beekeeping in Egypt having been dated to around 2400 BCE.

According to the traditions of Baka people, honey-gathering materials are made by men at the site at which the honey has been located. This type of basket is used for lowering honey found in trees to the ground below, sometimes from a height of 20 to 30 metres, using a strong liane (climbing vine) as a rope.

Basket, 1970s. Made by Baka people, Cameroon. Wood, leaf, raffia palm fibre. H. 46 cm, W. 17 cm, D. 27 cm. Af1979,15.58.

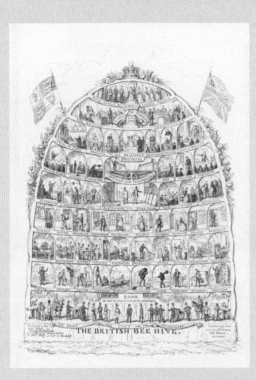

The idea of bee colonies as orderly, well-structured societies presided over by a queen bee has long fascinated people. Here, the illustrator and caricaturist George Cruikshank depicts British society as a beehive, with the monarchy at the apex.

George Cruikshank, *The British Bee Hive*, 1867. Published in London, UK. Etching on paper. H. 34.5 cm, W. 21 cm. 1869,1009.24.

An Egyptian wall-painting in the tomb of Rekhmire, for example, depicts the gathering of honey, including the use of smoke to pacify the bees. A similar practice is described by the first-century CE Roman writer Columella, who, in his treatise on agriculture, *De re rustica*, notes that smoke from the burning of dried dung was used to drive bees out of their hives so that their honey could be collected. The need to calm bees can be explained by the fact that the most-kept bee, the western honey bee (*Apis mellifera*), has the capacity to sting, which it does in defence of its honey. The wearing of protective clothing, including face coverings, when working with bees developed in Europe during the sixteenth century.

In countries around the world, beekeepers created hives for their bees using different, local materials, including earth, hollowed-out logs and calabashes. In Europe from around the fifth century BCE onwards, dome-shaped hives made from straw called skeps (from the Anglo-Saxon for 'basket') were especially popular. It was in North America, where the western honey bee had been introduced by European settlers in 1622, that a key hive innovation took place. In 1852, Reverend Lorenzo Langstroth patented his moveable-frame beehive. Langstroth's design allowed for easy access to the honeycomb without unduly disturbing the bees. It also enabled higher honey production per hive, and the Langstroth hive is widely used by beekeepers to this day.

Honey was highly valued, often seen as a food with divine origins and, in ancient Egypt, given as an offering in religious ceremonies. Today, honey is traded around the world, although honey fraud, in which honey is adulterated with sugar syrup, is a major concern among beekeepers.

GATHERING · FRUITS AND NUTS

Opposite: Mary Delany's paper collage shows *Fragaria vesca*, the wood or wild strawberry, whose tiny berries are prized for their intense flavour. Known collectively as the *Flora Delanica*, Delany's collages are appreciated not only for their beauty but also for their scientific accuracy.

Mary Delany, wood strawberry plant, 1777. UK. Collage of coloured papers, with body colour and watercolour, with black-ink background, on paper. H. 29.7 cm, W. 23 cm. 1897,0505.333. Bequeathed by Augusta Hall, Baroness Llanover.

Right, top: Nuts – edible seeds surrounded by a hard shell – are a remarkably nutritious food. The annual harvesting of such nuts as hazelnuts, almonds and chestnuts was an important part of gathering in stores for the winter.

Edward Henry Wehnert, *The Nut-Gatherers*, c. 1850. Published in London, UK. Woodcut print in colour on paper. H. 20.9 cm, W. 18.3 cm. 1918,1010.136. Donated by Campbell Dodgson.

Right, bottom: Chestnuts are a popular autumn food in Japan; chestnut purée is used in cakes, pastries and *wagashi* (traditional Japanese confections, often served with green tea). The appealing tactile quality of the chestnut is evident in this charming wooden netsuke (decorative toggle).

Netsuke of a monkey with two chestnuts, 19th century. Japan. Wood. H. 3.3 cm, W. 4.2 cm, D. 3.5 cm. HG.39. Donated by Professor John Hull Grundy and Anne Hull Grundy.

Fishing

More than 70 per cent of the Earth's surface is covered by water. In the quest to find food, humans learned to catch and gather the edible creatures that live in our planet's streams, rivers, ponds, lakes and seas, as well as on its shores. Fishing has been an important source of food for at least 10,000 years, and seafood continues to be widely caught and eaten in the present.

Over the centuries, communities have devised various ways of catching fish, including the use of harpoons or spears, the deployment of fish traps, and the digging of dams to capture fish. The fundamental pieces of fishing kit – the hook and line and the fishing net – have been used for thousands of years, and there is evidence of line-fishing using hooks, gorges and lightweight spears from at least 15,000 years ago. The gorge was a short piece of bone or wood sharpened to a point at each end; when a fish swallowed a baited gorge, the fisher pulled on the line, wedging the gorge in the fish's mouth. Early nets were woven from bark and other natural materials.

As people ventured out onto open water on rafts, canoes, coracles and sailing vessels, the practice of fishing from boats developed. Fishing at sea is a risky business, with storms among the perils faced by the fisher; commercial fishing remains one of the world's most dangerous industries. While fishing was originally a means of obtaining food, the skills and challenges involved in fishing and the thrill of the catch mean that angling has also long been enjoyed as a popular recreational sport.

Fresh fish is a very perishable food, so finding ways of preserving it was important. Salting and drying allowed large catches of fish caught out at sea, such as herring and cod, to be stored safely and transported. In Christian Europe, it was permitted to eat fish on fast days, when the consumption of meat was forbidden – a fact that ensured a large market for salted fish.

Historically, the Earth's oceans were regarded as providing a limitless supply of fish and were exploited accordingly. Sadly, however, fisheries around the world have been fished so intensively that their stocks have plummeted to the point of collapse. With wild stocks depleted, attention has turned to farming as a source of fish. Aquaculture, as such farming is known, was developed by the Chinese many centuries ago and was practised in Europe by the ancient Romans; during the medieval period, European monasteries and manor houses often had stew-ponds storing live fish, a useful resource in unstable times. Today, China is the world's largest producer of farmed seafood. There are, however, considerable environmental issues around fish farming, including contamination of the water with antibiotics and the spread of diseases from farmed to wild fish stocks. Furthermore, producing the fish meal that is fed to farmed fish adds to the already considerable pressure on wild fish stocks.

Opposite, top: Fish, both fresh and dried, was an important part of the Assyrian diet. The walls of the Neo-Assyrian Southwest Palace at Nineveh, built by the Assyrian king Sennacherib, were decorated with carved stone panels. Among the scenes depicted is this one of a man fishing in a mountain pool using a line.

Relief wall panel, 700–692 BCE. Nineveh, Iraq. Gypsum. H. 49.5 cm, W. 59 cm. 1897,1008.1. Donated by Miss H. G. Wainwright.

Opposite, bottom: *Ukai* is a traditional Japanese fishing method that uses trained cormorants. The birds are kept on leashes, while collars prevent them from eating the fish they catch. The cormorants are used specifically to catch *ayu* (sweetfish), a prized river fish.

Keisai Eisen, *Cormorant-fishing Boats on the Nagara River at Godo*, c. 1835–42. Japan. Colour woodblock print on paper. H. 23.1 cm, W. 35.7 cm. 1906,1220,0.974.

Below: Coastal societies in Peru have been using reed boats for transport and fishing for more than 3,000 years. In this reed-boat-shaped vessel, the two spouts have been replaced with the forms of two human figures. Motifs of fish and fishing nets can be seen on the vessel's body.

Vessel, 900–1400 CE. Pacasmayo, Peru. Pottery. H. 21 cm, W. 19 cm, Diam. 9 cm. Am1921,1027.28. Donated by J. H. Spottiswoode.

Below: Fishing out at sea is a dangerous way to make a living, even in the age of state-of-the-art fishing vessels equipped with electronic navigation devices. In this drawing, the ominous, looming presence of a storm threatens the two fishing vessels.

Joseph William Allen, two fishing boats in a storm, 1803–52. UK. Watercolour, touched with body colour, strengthened with gum, on paper. H. 17.9 cm, W. 23.5 cm. 1872,0113.361.

Right: In parts of Oceania, Pacific Islanders traditionally sought the blessings of the gods before setting out to sea. Fixed to canoes, such figures as this one are known as 'fisherman's gods'. Offerings were made to the figures to ensure a successful catch.

Figure, late 18th–early 19th century. Rarotonga, Cook Islands. Wood. H. 33 cm, W. 15.5 cm, D. 14 cm. Oc.9866. Donated by Sir Augustus Wollaston Franks.

Historically, whether a fisher would return with a good catch or not was partly down to chance. For this and other reasons, fishing has traditionally been seen as a financially risky way to make a living. This print shows a hopeful fisherman, envisioning a rewarding outing.

Unknown artist, fisherman observing the sea, 1475–81. Germany.
Hand-coloured woodcut on paper. H. 18.7 cm, W. 12.6 cm. 1895,1031.1081-1085.
Donated by Sir Augustus Wollaston Franks.

SHELLFISH

Together with fish, shellfish have long provided an important, aquatic source of food. The majority of the shellfish we eat are either molluscs or crustaceans. Unlike fish, shellfish are invertebrates, lacking backbones and internal skeletons. Many molluscs, including abalone, clams and scallops, have hard shells protecting their soft body parts (the word 'mollusc' derives from the Proto-Indo-European 'mel', meaning 'soft'). Cephalopods, such as squids and octopuses, are also categorized as molluscs. Crustaceans – crabs, crayfish and lobsters, for example – are members of the arthropod group, and are related to insects. They have a hard exoskeleton, or exterior skeleton, that protects their muscles and organs.

In addition to gathering molluscs from the sea and the seashore, some communities also learned how to farm them. The Romans, who considered oysters a great delicacy, created oyster beds; many of the beds that still exist in Britain were started by the Romans. Bivalve molluscs possess two hinged shells, which in some species can be tightly closed, enabling them to survive out of water for some time. This useful trait – from a human point of view – meant that bivalves, including oysters and mussels, could be transported. Oysters take several months to grow to market size. The flavour of oysters is directly influenced by the salinity of the water in which they live; the saltier it is, the more savoury they will taste. Mussels grow in clusters, attaching

Discovered in a Mycenaean chamber-tomb on the island of Rhodes, this krater is strikingly painted with an octopus on either side. The creatures' long, rippling tentacles are decorated with white dots. Octopus remains a popular food in Greece, especially on the islands.

Krater, 1375–1300 BCE. Greece. Pottery. H. 41 cm. 1959,1104.1.

themselves by special threads known as 'bysuss' to rocks or other supports. People took advantage of this natural characteristic to farm mussels by growing them on poles and ropes attached to rafts. Historically, cephalopods have been caught by a variety of fishing methods, including traps, baited lines and, in the case of the octopus, hunting with tridents or spears.

Traditionally, crabs and lobsters have been caught using baited pots; attracted by the bait, they venture into the pots and become trapped. Crustacean farming is a more recent development than the farming of molluscs; of all the crustaceans, it is the shrimp that is widely farmed. Today, shrimp aquaculture is big business, with shrimp the most valuable of all traded marine products.

From a culinary perspective, many shellfish are prized for their distinctive flavour and texture. It takes skill to cook shellfish well, since their delicate flesh can easily become dry and tough if overcooked. Around the world, one can find classic dishes from different cuisines that feature shellfish in a starring role: Greece's deep-fried kalamari, America's oysters Rockefeller, France's moules marinière, Italy's spaghetti alle vongole, Japan's prawn tempura, and Singapore's chilli crab. Shellfish can also be eaten raw: such dishes as freshly shucked oysters or scallop sashimi are enjoyed by many. Peru is famous for ceviche, a dish made by macerating finely sliced raw fish and shellfish in citrus juice or vinegar.

The inscription on this woodblock print includes an evocative image of plenty: 'On a summer's day / hot enough to set the calm / salt-sea to boiling, / the prawns of Shiba Bay / come bursting forth from their shells'.

Utagawa Hiroshige, spiny lobster and grey prawns, early 1830s. Japan. Colour woodblock print on paper. H. 25.3, W. 36.5 cm. 1906,1220,0.988. Bequeathed by Oscar Charles Raphael.

Above: The herring-buss was a seagoing fishing vessel, developed during the fifteenth century and widely used by Dutch and Flemish fishers. Long drift nets were employed to catch the abundant shoals of herring, while the freshly caught fish were preserved with salt while the boats were still at sea.

Adriaen van de Venne, a herring-buss on a calm sea, 1620–26. The Netherlands. Watercolour and body colour, over black chalk, heightened with silver, on paper. H. 9.6 cm, W. 15.2 cm. 1978,0624.42.42. Donated by HM Government.

Below: Images of fish and birds decorate this traditional fishing canoe from the Solomon Islands. There, bonito – medium-sized, tuna-like fishes of the family *Scombridae* – are highly sought-after. Fishers look for the flocks of birds that mass and dive into the shoals of fast-moving bonito, using the birds to guide them to a catch.

Canoe, 1962. Malatia, Solomon Islands. Wood, pearl shell, nut-putty. L. 408 cm. Oc1966,04.1.a-c. Donated by R. Spivey, through John Peake.

Above: Harbours, both natural and man-made, play an important part in the fishing industry. They offer a place where fishing boats can safely unload their catch and be sheltered from storms. This Constable drawing deftly captures the scene at Folkestone harbour in Kent.

John Constable, Folkestone harbour, 1833. UK. Pen and grey ink with watercolour on paper. H. 12.7 cm, W. 21 cm. 1888,0215.47. Donated by Isabel Constable.

Right: A frontispiece portrait of Isaac Walton, author of *The Compleat Angler*. First published in 1653, Walton's famous book is both a practical manual on angling and a poetic, pastoral discourse on the joys of fishing and the natural world.

Henry Robinson, *Honest Isaac Walton*, 1832. Published in London, UK. Etching and engraving on paper. H. 12.6 cm, W. 9.7 cm. 1861,0518.135.

Below: During the Vietnam War (1955–75), the Vietnamese artist and art teacher Nguyen Thu often took his students to the countryside to record what they saw. In this sketch, he depicts a soldier sitting with a bolt-action rifle propped beside him while he mends his damaged fishing net.

Drawing by Professor Nguyen Thu, 1965. Vietnam. Graphite on paper. H. 27.5 cm, W. 39 cm. 1999,0630,0.49.

Fish is an important foodstuff for Inuit, caught by various methods. This stone carving by the Inuit artist Jimmy Arnamissak shows a fisherman, equipped with both a fishing line and a harpoon, intent on catching his potential prey.

Figure, c. 1987. Made by Inuit artist Jimmy Inaruli Arnamissak in Inukjuaq, Canada. Stone, ivory, gut. H. 37.5 cm, W. 13.5 cm, D. 17 cm. Am1987,08.5.a-c.

COD

Once found in great abundance, the Atlantic cod (*Gadus morhea*) has played an important role in human history. An omnivorous feeder, with a preference for shallow water of around 37 metres or less, it is easily caught, a factor in its long popularity. Atlantic cod is found in sea waters from the Bay of Biscay to the Arctic, with its largest populations found in the northern part of that range.

It is in its preserved form, as salt cod or stockfish, that cod has been deeply significant. Salt cod is made by salting the fish (usually dry salting, rather than in brine), then drying it. Stockfish, made in Norway since the Viking era, is produced simply by drying cod in cold air without an initial salting stage. The salting and drying processes drive out moisture, transforming what was a fresh, highly perishable item into a long-lasting, durable, protein-rich food that can be transported successfully over long distances.

In Christian Europe, the religious calendar included numerous fast days, during which it was forbidden to eat meat. Fish was permitted, however, and from the early medieval period salt cod became the preferred food for fast days. In Spain and Portugal, both Catholic countries, it is notable that the word for 'cod' is the same as the word for 'salt cod', since the latter, rather than the fresh fish, is what is widely eaten.

The lucrative demand for cod saw people seek out fresh stocks of the fish to transform into salt cod. The Icelandic coast had long been a source of cod for European fishers. In 1497, on an expedition for Henry VII

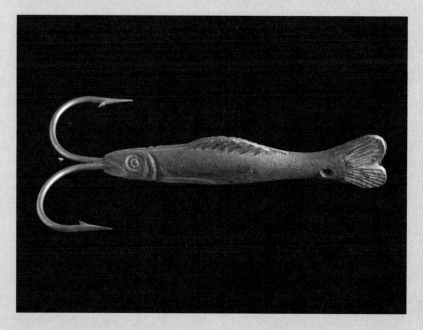

This cod-shaped fish hook recalls Newfoundland's fishing history. Cod fish were once abundant off Newfoundland's coast. Overfishing, however, saw the collapse of the fishery and led to the introduction in the 1990s of an ongoing moratorium on commercial cod fishing.

Fish hook, c. 2000. Newfoundland, Canada. Lead, steel. H. 20 cm, W. 11 cm. Am2002,04.5. Purchased from Craft Council of Newfoundland and Labrador, funded by the Sosland Foundation.

In British cities and towns, 'wet fish' was traditionally sold by costermongers. Judging by the suspicious expression on the customer's face in this print by George Belcher, the fish head she is being offered does not live up to the print's title.

George Belcher, *Fresh Cod*, 1922. UK. Coloured etching on paper. H. 29.8 cm, W. 23.8 cm. 1925,0302.1. Donated by George Belcher.

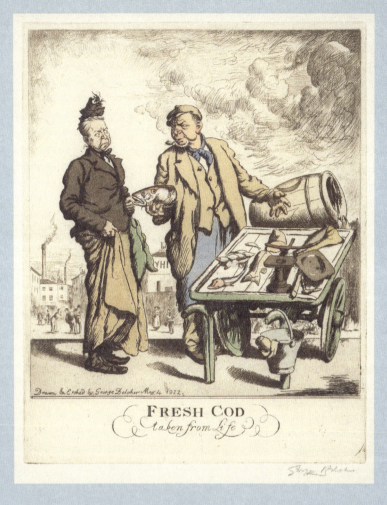

of England to seek out a new sea route for the spice trade, the explorer Giovanni Caboto, also known as John Cabot, 'discovered' the huge island of Newfoundland, off the North American coast. He reported back that the waters were teeming with codfish. To the southeast of Newfoundland are a series of underwater plateaus known as the Grand Banks. The nutrient-rich waters around the banks are naturally abundant in krill and small fish, offering plentiful food for cod. The fish was found here in a far greater density than in European fisheries, and extensive cod fishing off the Grand Banks ensued, lasting for centuries. Due to chronic overfishing, however, the cod stocks fell catastrophically, and in 1992 a moratorium on cod fishing in the area was announced, extended indefinitely in 1994.

Because salt cod could be transported and traded around the world, it can be found in a number of cuisines. Classic dishes featuring the ingredient include Jamaica's saltfish and ackee, France's brandade, Portugal's *pasteis de bacalhau* (salt cod fritters) and, from the Basque region of Spain, *bacalao a la vizcaina*. Salt cod plays a particularly extensive part in Portuguese cuisine, where it is known as *fiel amigo* (faithful friend). Owing to low fish stocks, cod, once a cheap, plentiful food, is increasingly an expensive treat.

Left: In Roman mythology, Neptune was the god of water and the sea. In this charming image, an infant Neptune is riding a sea creature through the waves while attendant putti offer him platters piled, fittingly, with seafood and coral.

Jonas Umbach, infant Neptune riding a sea creature, 1645–1700. Germany. Etching on paper. H. 7.4 cm, W. 9 cm. 1870,0625.501.

Opposite, top: Roman mosaics, made from tesserae (small cubes of stone, ceramic or glass), were a symbol of wealth and status. Edible fish and seafood, including an octopus, from the Mediterranean area are represented in this panel from a mosaic floor, which probably decorated a dining room.

Mosaic floor panel, c. 100 CE. Said to be from Populonia, Italy. Stone. H. 88.9 cm, W. 101.14 cm. 1989,0322.1.

Below: This Japanese handscroll is an example of a *gassaku*, a collaborative work of art often created in a social setting, such as a party. Twelve artists took turns to paint fish and other seafood, displaying an impressive knowledge of different species. The increasingly loose style of the painting suggests that the artists were drinking *sake* while working on the scroll.

Suzuki Shonen, Sakurai Hyakurei, Imao Keinen, Suzuki Hyakunen, Nishida Chikusen, Oyabu Kodo, Izawa Kyuko, Mokusen, Rankei, Suzuki Hyakusui, Hishida Nitto and Kubota Beisen, a variety of seafood, 1870–73. Japan. Painted paper handscroll. H. 32 cm, W. 679.1 cm. 1991,0701,0.1.

Far right: This fishing lure is made from bamboo and shaped like a scoop. The lure was dropped into the water by bonito fishers, causing splashes that attracted the bonito by simulating the activity of small bait fish.

Lure, c. 1880–1902. New Georgia Island, Solomon Islands. Bamboo. H. 24.5 cm, W. 4.8 cm, D. 5.1 cm. Oc1902,0603.14. Donated by Charles M. Woodford.

Right: Inuit use every part of the animals they hunt and kill. Walruses provide meat and blubber for food, hides from which to make canoes or rope and, from their tusks, ivory to shape into jewelry, carvings or fish hooks.

Fish hook, 19th century. Made by Aleut or Inupiaq, Alaska, USA. Walrus ivory, iron, cork. H. 9.8 cm, W. 2 cm, D. 3 cm. Am1890,0908.133. Donated by Hugh Cecil Lowther, 5th Earl of Lonsdale.

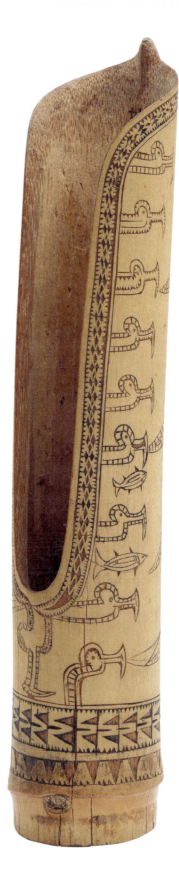

Fishing with spears, harpoons and hooks was commonplace in late Ice Age Europe. Line fishing using small barbed points as fish hooks was practised about 14,000 years ago. Images of fish on fishing equipment, weapons and cave walls occur around this time, suggesting that fish were an important part of the hunter-gatherer diet.

Fish hooks, 14,000 years ago. Courbet Cave, France. Antler. H. 4.6–7.2 cm, W. 0.7–2.2 cm, D. 0.3–0.7 cm. 1864,1226.569, 1864,1226.574-578.

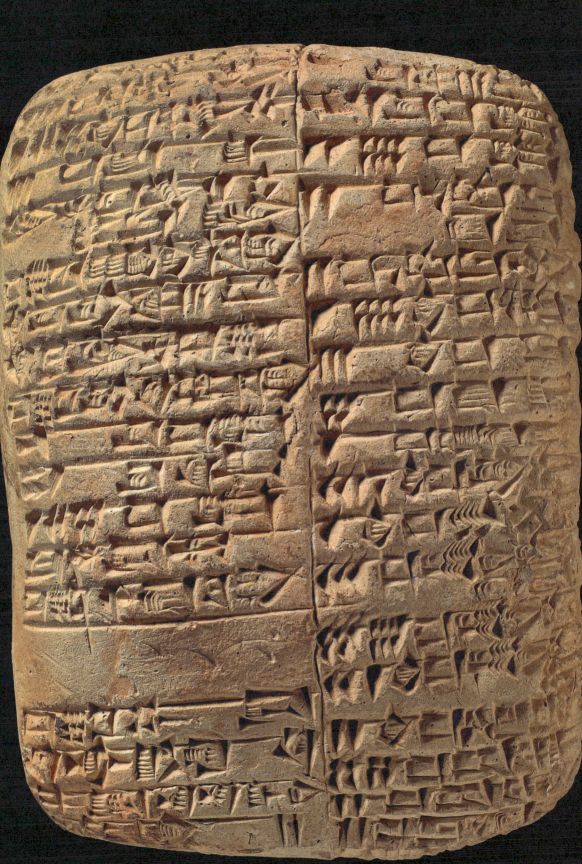

Agriculture: plants

About 12,000 years ago, communities in various parts of the world began to move away from a hunter-gatherer lifestyle towards an agrarian one, in which people grew crops and kept animals for food. This shift was a gradual, diverse and complex process, and there are different theories as to why and how it occurred. Climate change is thought to be a factor. Towards the end of the last Ice Age, around 12,000 years ago, temperatures began to rise and glaciers started to melt; in the Middle East, the ecological changes caused by this warming are believed to have encouraged a slow transition to agriculture. An increase in the demand for food driven by rising populations is considered another possible cause. Hunter-gatherer communities had already managed plants and animals in a number of ways, including cultivation. It is thought that those sedentary hunter-gatherer groups who had settled close to an ample food source began planting the seeds of wild grains, as well as gathering them. With the planting of crops came the need to harvest them when they were ready; this cycle of sowing, tending and reaping thus gave shape to a new way of living.

The rise of farming saw people living in permanent settlements. Farming, however, was far from being an easy alternative to hunting and gathering. Among its challenges were the hard physical labour required to work the land and the threat of losing crops to bad weather or pests. Archaeological evidence suggests that, in comparison to hunter-gatherers, farmers were less healthy. Their diet was far less varied than that of foragers, and they suffered from malnutrition. Farming communities, with their larger populations and close proximity to livestock, were also prone to diseases and parasites. Despite its difficulties, however, agriculture was more productive than hunter-gathering, producing more food per unit of territory and creating food surpluses. This increased supply of food allowed the human population to grow substantially. In about 10,000 BCE, there were between 5 and 8 million people on Earth; by the first century BCE, the world's population had risen to 250 million and farming was the predominant way of life. Villages grew into towns and then cities.

Cereals play a major part in the story of agriculture, becoming staple foods in many parts of the world. Grains could be dried and stored and were an important source of calories; their by-products, chaff and straw, were used for fuel, animal fodder and construction. As people began to cultivate grains, they favoured plants that, owing to a genetic mutation, had non-shattering grains (that is, seeds that did *not* disperse on ripening), making it far easier to harvest them. Today, we still depend on cereals to sustain us: according to the United Nations' Food and Agriculture Organization, 60 per cent of the world's energy intake comes from just three grains: wheat, rice and maize.

After the Russian Revolution, undecorated porcelain plates from the Imperial Porcelain Factory in St Petersburg were given designs promoting the ideology of the new Communist regime. This design of a farmer sowing seed celebrated the value of such essential labour and the strength of people formerly disregarded as insignificant peasants.

Plate, from the Imperial Porcelain Factory, 1919. St Petersburg, Russia. Porcelain. Diam. 24.4 cm, D. 2.6 cm. 2000,0904.1.

Above: Rice is a staple food in Japan. Growing the rice, however, is a labour-intensive affair. Historically, the young rice seedlings were transplanted from their seedbed to a rice paddy, planted in neat rows by hand. This work was traditionally done by women.

Katsushika Hokusai, scene of rice planting, 1790s–1810s. Japan. Colour woodblock print on paper. H. 25.7 cm, W. 37.9 cm. 1945,1101,0.50.

Right: A rural scene of ploughing and sowing in Ethiopia. One of the staple crops long cultivated in the country is a small-seeded grain called teff. Teff is grown not only for its edible seeds, but also for straw to use as fodder; its flour is used to make injera, a fermented, pancake-like flatbread.

Painting, 1960s. Ethiopia. Watercolour on parchment. H. 22.2 cm, W. 26.8 cm. Af1969,33.9. From Mrs Assegey Asefa.

RICE

Rice is one of humanity's most important foods, a staple for around half of the world's population. It is a calorific cereal, producing more energy and protein per acre than either wheat or maize, and therefore supporting more people per unit of land than these other staples. Rice is a member of the grass family (Gramineae), belonging to the genus *Oryza*. In addition to several wild species, the genus includes two cultivated species: *Oryza sativa*, which is grown commercially on all continents apart from Antarctica, and *Oryza glaberrima*, which grows in West Africa. Initially, it was wild rice that was gathered for its edible seeds and then planted; eventually, this process led to cultivated rice. A key difference between the two is that while wild rice naturally sheds its seeds as they ripen (a process called seed shattering), cultivated rice retains its seeds, making it easier to harvest.

Oryza sativa was first domesticated in Asia, although exactly where is disputed. Remains of the plant have been discovered at the Neolithic Hemudu site in the Yangtze River valley, confirming China's long relationship with rice. The legendary Chinese emperor Shennong, known also as 'the Emperor of the Five Grains', is said to have taught the Chinese how to grow rice. Nowadays, China both produces and consumes the most rice in the world. Of the two cultivated species, it is *Oryza sativa* that has spread around the globe, transported largely by humans, who carried the small, portable grains for food and trade. From Asia, rice spread via Persia into Europe. The Moors grew rice in Spain and Sicily, with the Spanish and the Portuguese introducing rice to the Americas in the sixteenth and seventeenth centuries.

Rice occupies a central place in Chinese cuisine. The traditional Chinese greeting '*Chi fan le mei you?*' translates literally as 'Have you eaten your grain yet?' In Chinese tableware, the 'rice grain pattern', with its translucent forms in the shape of grains of rice, remains popular today and is widely used in blue-and-white bowls.

Bowl, *c.* 1800. China. Glazed porcelain. H. 6.4 cm, Diam. 14.2 cm. Franks.727.+. Donated by Sir Augustus Wollaston Franks.

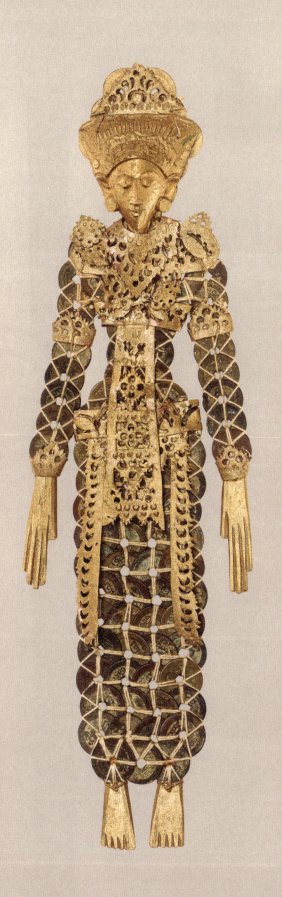

Rice is a versatile, semi-aquatic plant, able to grow in a range of environments, from hillsides ('upland rice') to areas prone to flooding ('floating rice'). It was rice's capacity to produce good yields when grown in shallow, slow-moving water that led to it being cultivated this way, using specially created irrigation systems. Flooding the rice fields both reduces pests and weeds and brings nutrients to the plants. Once harvested, the 'paddy' – as rough or unhusked rice is called – has to be threshed, dried and milled. Milling removes the husk and bran layers, producing an edible white kernel.

From a culinary point of view, it is useful to know that there are two recognized sub-species of *Oryza sativa*, and that each one produces a different result when cooked. *Indica* rice, of which basmati is an example, is characterized by long grains with a high content of amylose starch, which produces firm, separate grains. *Japonica* rice, by contrast, has shorter grains with a far lower amylose starch content, resulting in sticky grains that clump together. *Japonicas* come in short- and medium-grain varieties. The latter, such as Arborio, are used for risottos, while both types can be used for sushi.

Dewi Sri, the goddess of rice and fertility, is still worshipped in many parts of South and Southeast Asia. An Indonesian legend tells how a woman called Samyan Sri was raised by the gods, but then killed by them when her beauty threatened the harmony of the heavens. The rice plant grew from her buried body, and she was elevated to a goddess, becoming Dewi Sri.

Figure, 1950s. Bali, Indonesia. Metal, pottery, paper, wood, fibre. H. 45 cm, W. 10 cm, D. 25 cm. As1994,20.3. Donated by Professor Eila M. J. Campbell.

Rice is the most widely cultivated food in Southeast Asia, and protecting the rice crop is of great importance. In Vietnam, anthropomorphic guardian figures, such as this one made from vegetable fibre and bamboo, were set in rice fields to scare off birds and ward off evil spirits.

Guardian figure, mid-20th century. Giê peoples, Vietnam. Bamboo, vegetable fibre. H. 121 cm, W. 110 cm, D. 1.7 cm. As1956,06.1.

Yams, a type of tuber, have long been part of the diet of the Indigenous Kanak people of New Caledonia. In the past, stones infused with magical powers were placed in the ground with the crops to help ensure a plentiful harvest.

Magic stone, 19th century. Lifou, New Caledonia. Stone. H. 2.5 cm, W. 2.5 cm, L. 12.5 cm. Oc1944,02.1131. Donated by Irene Marguerite Beasley.

This Botticelli drawing of a female figure is thought to represent either Abundance or Autumn, the season of harvest. The woman is accompanied by putti, one of which holds a cornucopia, the symbol of plenty, another a bunch of grapes.

Sandro Botticelli, *Abundance* or *Autumn*, c. 1480–85. Italy. Pen, brown ink and brown wash on paper. H. 31.7 cm, W. 25.2 cm. 1895,0915.447.

WHEAT

Wheat was one of the first plants to be cultivated. Today, this cereal grain is a staple crop for millions, grown for its edible seed on more land than any other commercial crop, and an important source of calories for around 20 per cent of the world's population. The domestication of wheat has played an important role in human history. The shift from gathering roots, fruits and grains to cultivating them changed ways of life, encouraging settlement and supporting larger populations.

Wheat is a grass of the genus *Triticum*, descended from wild grass, and its origins can be traced to the Near East. A site near Jericho in the Jordan Valley shows evidence of two early domesticated wheats, einkorn and emmer. The seed heads of domesticated wheat, unlike those of wild wheat, do not shatter when ripe, enabling productive harvesting to take place. Wheat cultivation spread from the Near East to Europe (where it was an important crop for the Romans), Africa and South Asia. European colonists introduced wheat to the Americas. One reason for its prominence as a food crop is that wheat can be grown in a variety of soils and climates. Many countries grow wheat, with China, India, Russia, the United States, France, Canada, Pakistan and Ukraine among the world's major producers.

Opposite: Issued by the Assembly of Philadelphia in 1781, during the American War of Independence (1775–83), this banknote offers a reassuring image of peaceful prosperity, depicting a plough on a field and, representing the results of harvest, three neatly tied wheatsheaves.

Banknote, 1781. Issued in Pennsylvania, USA. Paper. H. 8.9 cm, W. 6.7 cm. 1984,0605.1598.

Right: Historically, cereal grains provided a vital source of food for millions of people. In some countries, grains came to represent wealth, often appearing on coins and banknotes. On both sides of this Aksumite gold coin is a head – crowned on one side – flanked by two stalks of wheat.

Coin, c. 340–540 CE. Minted in Aksum, Ethiopia. Gold. Diam. 1.7 cm, 1.6 g. OR.3505.

The flour milled from wheat is widely used to make bread, cakes and pastries. Wheat is prized for its gluten content, which allows for the successful baking of raised breads and cakes. Most of the wheat that is grown today is a cultivar of the species *T. aestivum*, the type of wheat used for making bread. The term 'hardness' is used to describe protein and gluten levels, which vary among wheat varieties. When it comes to baking, different flours lend themselves to different uses depending on these levels. 'Strong' white flour, for example, is excellent for making bread, being tolerant of over-kneading. The flour used for cakes is generally milled from softer types of wheat.

As well as bread, wheat is used to make pasta and couscous, two other food staples. The wheat variety used for these purposes is *T. durum*, which has an especially tough grain (hence 'durum', which is derived from the Latin for 'hard'). The flour produced from the grain of durum wheat is known as semolina and has a characteristically coarse texture owing to the grain's hardness. Durum wheat not only has a high gluten content, but the gluten itself is less elastic than bread-wheat gluten, which makes it easier to roll out and shape.

Above, top: The gathering-in of hay, made from dried grass, to provide feed for livestock through the winter remains an important event in the agricultural year. Prior to the introduction of mechanized farming, it took a lot of labour to harvest the hay and was often a communal effort.

Drawing, by Randolph Caldecott, 1846–86. UK. Watercolour, touched with body colour, on paper. H. 13.8 cm, W. 25.1 cm. 1886,0619.349.

Above: The work of the British artist Samuel Palmer is characterized by images of an idealized pastoral life. Painted while he was living in the village of Shoreham, Kent, this night-time scene of a farmer walking through a field of harvested grain is invested with a poetic mystery.

Samuel Palmer, *Cornfield by Midnight, with the Evening Star*, c. 1830. UK. Watercolour and body colour, with pen and ink on paper. H. 19.7 cm, W. 29.8 cm. 1985,0504.1. Purchased with contribution from National Heritage Memorial Fund, Henry Moore Foundation, the British Museum Company, British Museum Friends (as British Museum Society) and Sir Duncan Oppenheim.

In the agricultural calendar, the harvest season is when the hard labour of sowing and tending crops is rewarded. These painted and enamelled Limoges plaques, showing grapes being turned into wine and farm workers taking a break from harvesting the ripe grain to eat and drink together, convey a sense of plenty.

Plaques, from the workshop of Jean Pénicaud II, c. 1555. Limoges, France. Copper, enamel, gold. H. 4.5–4.6 cm, W. 9 cm. 1902,1117.1–2.

Below: Kitchen gardens range from large, orderly walled affairs, attached to great houses and designed to feed their households, to small, less formal but equally productive plots. One of the rewards they offer for the effort they require is the enjoyment of truly fresh produce.

William Small, digging potatoes in a kitchen garden, 1871. UK. Watercolour strengthened with gum on paper with strip added at left. H. 27.6 cm, W. 40.5 cm. 1997,0712.112.

Opposite, top: The perennial struggle between growers defending their crops and pests eager to eat them provided inspiration for the artist Beatrix Potter. Among her bestselling children's books are the adventures of Peter Rabbit, Benjamin Bunny and the Flopsy Bunnies as they outwit Mr McGregor, the gardener.

Beatrix Potter, rabbits eating lettuce leaves: illustration for *The Tale of the Flopsy Bunnies*, 1909. UK. Pen and brown ink and watercolour on paper. H. 9.1 cm, W. 10.4 cm. 1946,1121.8. Donated by Capt. Kenneth Duke.

Opposite, bottom: As any gardener will tell you, gardens need looking after in order to thrive. Edward Bawden depicts a diligent gardener, concentrating on his work. The ripe apples overhead and the bright red tomatoes show the fruits of his labour.

Edward Bawden, *Autumn*, 1950. UK. Colour linocut on paper. H. 38 cm, W. 50.5 cm. 1951,0407.6. Donated by Shrimpton & Giles Fund.

MAIZE

Another of the world's major food staples, maize (*Zea mays*), also known as corn, originated in Mesoamerica. It is generally thought to be descended from a wild grass called teosinte (*Zea spp.*), with Mexico considered its primary centre of domestication. The earliest known corn remains were found in Mexico, in the Guilá Naquitz cave, Oaxaca, and have been dated to 6,250 years ago.

Many varieties of maize are grown today. Their kernels vary in both colour – white, yellow, red, purple, black, speckled – and size. The different types of maize are categorized according to their starch content and appearance. Flint corn, as its name suggests, is distinguished by its stony hardness, owing to its high starch content. The corn used to make popcorn is a type of flint corn. When heated, the natural moisture inside popcorn kernels turns to steam and the pressure causes the endosperm, the starchy material in the middle of the grain, to explode. Dent corn – named for its appearance when dried – has softer kernels. Flour corns, which include blue corns, are soft and easy to grind. Sweetcorn has more sugar than starch and is eaten when immature. One striking development after centuries of plant breeding is that, unlike other grains, maize cannot propagate itself. The protective husk around the tightly packed kernels prevents this.

The *Popol Vuh*, the sacred Maya text, tells of how the gods created the first humans out of maize – a staple crop for the Maya. This carving depicts the Young Maize God on his emergence from the Underworld as the embodiment of vitality and new growth.

Sculpture, 715 CE. Copan, Honduras. Limestone. H. 89 cm, W. 56.5 cm, D. 30 cm. Am1923,Maud.8. Donated by Alfred Maudslay.

In ancient Mesoamerican civilizations – including the Maya and the Aztec – maize was hugely important culturally, featuring in creation myths. Many varieties of maize were grown in Mesoamerica, where it was eaten as a food and consumed in drinks. In the Andes it was also fermented to make maize beer, known as chicha, which was used for libations.

Pre-colonial Mesoamerican and Andean societies developed a way of treating maize to make it more digestible. Known as nixtamalization, from the Nahuatl *nextli*, meaning 'ashes', the process involves soaking dried corn in an alkali solution – water mixed with ash, crushed limestone or seashells – in order to remove the fibrous skins from the kernels. Not only is nixtamalized corn more digestible, it also increases its nutritional value, making the small amount of niacin (an essential human nutrient) in corn more easily absorbed by the body. Nixtamalized corn is an important ingredient in Latin American cuisine. It is ground, traditionally using a type of stone quern called a metate, and kneaded with water to make a dough called *masa*, from which corn tortillas and tamales are made.

From Mesoamerica, maize was introduced into other regions of the world, with Christopher Columbus credited with bringing it to Spain, and Portuguese and Arab traders introducing it to Africa. When corn was adopted as a staple food in other countries by deprived communities who lacked the knowledge of nixtamalization, they tended to suffer from pellagra, a disease caused by a lack of niacin. While maize is consumed as food in many parts of the world, it is also used to feed livestock – notably in the United States – and in non-food-based manufacturing, including the production of corn-starch plastic and ethanol.

For Hopi people of northern Arizona, kachinas are the spirits in the world around them. Kachina dolls are representations of these spirits, designed to be given to Hopi children. This kachina doll, carved from cottonwood root, is in the form of two corn maidens, who symbolize prayers for a bountiful corn harvest and personify fertility and growth.

Kachina doll, 1996. Made by Derrick Davis, Hopi and Choctaw Nations, Arizona, USA. Cottonwood, metal, feather. H. 80 cm, W. 25 cm, D. 25 cm. Am1996,13.1.

Above: In ancient Egypt, grain was the main ingredient in two dietary staples: beer and bread. The Rhind Mathematical Papyrus contains a selection of mathematical problems and is thought to have been used for teaching mathematics. Among the problems is how to calculate the amount of grain that could be stored in a cylindrical granary.

Papyrus, Second Intermediate Period, c. 1550 BCE. Thebes, Egypt. Papyrus. H. 33 cm, W. 296 cm. EA 10057.

Below: The simplest form of winnowing – the process of separating the chaff from the grain – involves tossing grain into the air so that the lighter chaff is blown away while the heavier grain falls back down. This winnowing tray from Sarawak is made from rattan, bamboo and sap.

Winnowing trays, 1986–87. Made by Tepo Ben, Merua' Ulun and Unid Tala from Kelabit communities, Borneo. Rattan, bamboo, sap. H. 16.4–16.7 cm, W. 47.2–49.5 cm, D. 55–56 cm. As1988,22.89, As1988,22.90. Donated by Dr Monica Janowski.

Right: The fact that buckwheat grows quickly, even in unfavourable conditions, producing crops of its edible seeds two or three times a year, makes it a valued food plant. In Brittany, buckwheat flour is traditionally used to make galettes, or savoury crêpes.

Frédéric Laguillermie, *Jeune bretonne vannant du blé noir au bord de la mer* (Young Breton Woman Winnowing Buckwheat by the Sea), *c.* 1874. France. Etching on paper. H. 17.9 cm, W. 12.8 cm. 1878,0511.159.

CITRUS

Oranges, lemons, grapefruits, limes, satsumas … the citrus family offers a wide range of fruits for us to enjoy. One reason for the rich variety of fruits within the genus *Citrus* is the plant's capacity to hybridize. Natural crossing and mutations in the wild, together with centuries of selective breeding, make unravelling the relationships between citrus species and varieties a complex matter. Five wild ancestral species, however, have been identified. The citrus is native to a large portion of the world, extending from Australia in the south to China in the north, with its ancestry thought to stretch back more than 20 million years. In India, a collection of religious texts called the *Vajasaneyi Samhita*, dating from before 800 BCE, mentions the lemon (*Citrus × limon*) and the citron (*Citrus medica*). Han Yanzhi's *Ju lu* (Record of Citrus), an early Chinese account of citrus cultivation written in 1178 CE, records twenty-seven varieties of citrus fruits and provides instructions on how to grow them.

Historically, citrus fruits were valued for their fragrance and for their medicinal, magical and religious properties. The citron (known in Hebrew as *etrog*) is used in the Jewish festival of Sukkot. It spread from Asia to Persia and from there was the first citrus fruit to reach Europe. Other citrus fruits were spread around the globe through trade and conquest. Following Christopher Columbus's voyages, the sweet orange (*Citrus × aurantium*) was taken from Europe to the New World; reports exist of the Spanish growing oranges in Florida in 1565. The grapefruit (*Citrus paradisi*), a cross between the sweet orange and the pomelo, originated in the West Indies in the eighteenth century.

In China, the distinctively shaped and intensely fragrant citrus fruit known as the Buddha's hand fruit (*fo shou*) is a symbol of happiness, longevity and good fortune. Offered to household gods as a New Year gift, it is often depicted in Chinese art, from paintings to jade carvings.

Gao You, *Buddha's Hand Fruit*, from the *Ten Bamboo Studio Collection of Calligraphy and Painting*, c. 1633. Nanjing, China. Woodblock print on paper. H. 25 cm, W. 27 cm. 1930,0319,0.1.

The German botanical artist and scholar of the natural world Maria Sibylla Merian is famed for the drawings she made during a trip to Suriname in South America at the end of the seventeenth century. This characteristically detailed example depicts the bitter orange, together with the silk-moth caterpillar and butterfly.

Maria Sibylla Merian, a branch of the bitter orange tree, c. 1701–05. Germany. Watercolour and body colour, heightened with white, and with pen and grey ink, on vellum. H. 37.7 cm, W. 26.5 cm. SL,5275.52. Bequeathed by Sir Hans Sloane.

In culinary terms, citrus fruits are prized for their fragrance, their natural acidity (owing to the presence of citric acid) and their juice, contained within tiny, fluid-filled structures called vesicles. The fruits can be used in the kitchen in numerous ways: in refreshing salads and desserts, for example, or to flavour sauces in such dishes as duck à l'orange. In Morocco, salt-preserved lemons are used as a flavouring for tagines and other dishes; in Iran and Iraq, dried limes add a musky citrus note to stews. Citrus peel, with its aromatic zest rich in volatile oils, is prized in its own right. The chopped peel of bitter Seville oranges is transformed into marmalade, bergamot oil is used to perfume Earl Grey tea, and the peel of citron, oranges and lemons is candied and used to flavour pastries, cakes and other sweet creations.

Today, the sweet orange is the most commonly cultivated of all the citrus fruits, with Brazil, the European Union and China among the largest growers by volume of fruit produced. Most of this crop is turned into orange juice, valued not just for its taste but because it is rich in Vitamin C.

Cuneiform (meaning 'wedge-shaped') characters were imprinted on damp clay tablets using a stylus. Many of the earliest cuneiform texts are records of goods. This tablet, dating from the Third Dynasty of Ur, is a record of orchards, including the number of fruit trees and the names of the gardeners.

Tablet, 2100–2000 BCE. Southern Iraq. Clay. H. 9.8 cm, W. 7.3 cm. 1896,0406.7.

The peach occupies a special place in Chinese culture, symbolizing immortality and longevity. In Chinese mythology, the Peaches of Immortality conferred the gift of eternal life on those who ate them. Peaches are a popular subject, with the peach trees on this dish shown both flowering and fruiting.

Dish, 1723–35. Jingdezhen, China. Porcelain. H. 8.9 cm, Diam. 50.7 cm. PDF,A.840. On loan to the British Museum from the Sir Percival David Collection.

Right, top: Fruit has long been prized not only for its flavour but also for its aesthetic qualities. In this Dutch still life, the artist combines medlars, a bunch of grapes and raspberries with an assortment of colourful flowers to create an image of plenty.

Jan van Os, study of flowers and fruit by a vase, 1759–1808. The Netherlands. Watercolour, partly strengthened by gum, on paper. H. 37.4 cm, W. 29.2 cm. 1895,0915.1231.

Right, bottom: The pineapple became an exotic status symbol in Europe during the seventeenth and eighteenth centuries. Here, Charles II of England is shown being presented by his gardener with what was claimed to be the first pineapple grown in the country.

Robert Graves, King Charles II receiving a pineapple, 1823. Published in London, UK. Etching and engraving on paper. H. 34 cm, W. 39.3 cm. 1871,1209.1466.

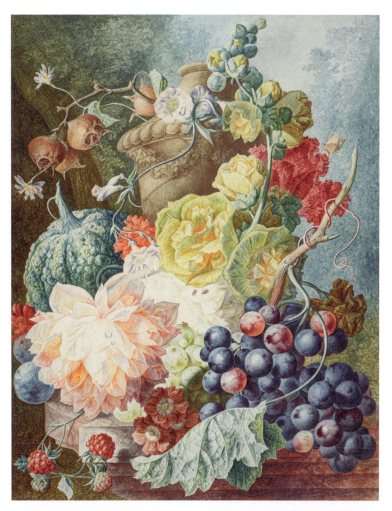

Agriculture: animals

Together with the cultivation of plants, the domestication of wild animals, such as goats and cattle, was central to the development of agriculture. While the world is home to more than a hundred large, terrestrial, herbivorous mammals, only fourteen have been domesticated. Of these, five in particular have played an important role: sheep, goats, cattle, pigs and horses. It is thought that the domestication of animals may have had its origins in selective hunting, with hunters sparing the females or the young, and then protecting them from other predators. Most of the livestock animals used in farming today were domesticated thousands of years ago. Domesticating wild animals involved a process of selective breeding, with people choosing animals for desirable or useful traits, including docility or plumpness; over the generations, these traits were passed down. Such has been the extent of human selection that domestic animals have different skeletal elements and teeth from their wild ancestors and are now dependent on humans. Over the centuries, certain livestock animals have been bred for a particular purpose. The Holstein cow, for example, is thought to have first been selected for dairy qualities about 2,000 years ago; today, it is known for its high milk yield, producing on average 10,122 litres of milk each lactation.

In addition to rearing livestock for their meat, hides and bones, people have found many other uses for domestic animals while they are alive. The milk from such animals as goats, sheep and cattle is valued as a nutritious drink and the starting point for the production of protein-rich dairy foods, including cheese, butter and yoghurt. Chickens, of course, provide eggs as well as meat. The manure produced by animals like cattle and pigs is used as a fertilizer to enrich the soil in which crops are grown. Domestic livestock has also long been set to work for humans. Horses, camels, donkeys, llamas and oxen have been used for farm work, like pulling ploughs, turning grinding stones and raising water from wells. Before the advent of the train and the motor car, they were also vital sources of transport, carrying both goods and people.

In certain arid regions of the world, communities learned to live off their herds, developing a pastoralist lifestyle. In contrast to farmers who lived settled lives, tending the land and their animals, pastoralists were nomadic, moving their livestock in the quest to find fresh sources of pasture on which to graze them. The pastoral way of life still carries on today – in the Sahel region of Western and Central Africa, for example, and among Sami people of Scandinavia, who herd reindeer.

The twentieth century saw the industrialization of livestock farming, with such animals as battery hens kept in small spaces. Whereas meat was historically a luxury in many countries, intensive large-scale farming has made it affordable and widely available. Global consumption of meat has increased over the past few decades and, despite concerns over the environmental impact of eating meat, demand is predicted to rise.

Opposite: These engravings are known as the 'Crying Cows'. As sunlight moves across them, the long-horned cattle they depict appear to move. When the rains come, water collects at the base of the engravings, creating the illusion that the animals are bending their heads to drink it.

Photograph, David Coulson MBE, 1997. Carvings 7,000–8,000 years old. Tegharghart, Algeria. 2013,2034.4328. Donated by Trust for African Rock Art.

Below: In Oceania, pigs are one of a limited number of indigenous mammals and are highly prized by Islanders. In New Guinea, they are presented as gifts at ceremonies, or as payments in marriage settlements. Every part of the pig is valued, including its tusks, which are worn as ornaments.

Bowl, before 1872. Admiralty Islands, Papua New Guinea. Wood. H. 13.5 cm, W. 15 cm, D. 39.5 cm. Oc.7844. Donated by Sir Augustus Wollaston Franks.

Right: In addition to being pack animals, llamas are an important source of meat and wool for South America's altiplano communities. During the Inca period, miniature golden llamas were left as offerings alongside high-altitude human sacrifices to the mountain gods intended to ensure the vital replenishment of the altiplano grasses.

Figurine, 1400–1532. Peru. Gold. H. 6.5 cm, W. 1.1 cm, D. 5.9 cm. Am1921,0721.1.

AGRICULTURE: ANIMALS · LIVESTOCK

SHEEP

The domestic sheep (*Ovis aries*) is thought to have been domesticated from a wild sheep (*Ovis orientalis*) by around 9000 BCE in a region in the Middle East known as the 'Fertile Crescent'. Certain innate aspects of sheep, such as the fact that they are timid, gregarious animals, with a tendency to follow a dominant leader, as well as lacking strong territorial instincts, are assumed to have aided the domestication process. Wild sheep have hairy coats rather than wool; the now characteristic woolly fleece of the domestic sheep is something that developed through breeding.

As ruminants, sheep feed on grass and shrubs. From a farming perspective, they possess the useful quality of being able to survive in a wide range of climates and habitats, ranging from cold, wet mountains to hot, dry regions. Once domesticated, sheep spread into many parts of the world, including Europe, North Africa and Asia.

When it comes to sheep husbandry, there is a long pastoral tradition. Flocks of sheep, tended by a shepherd and a sheep dog to guard against predators, were kept outdoors on grazing grounds; sometimes, they were moved from area to area in a seasonal cycle in order to find fresh food. This way of keeping sheep is still practised in certain regions of the world, including the Middle East, North Africa and Central Asia.

Sheep have many uses, making them practical animals to keep. They are valued for their meat, their hides, their warm wool, which can be woven into cloth, and their milk, which can be drunk or turned into yoghurt or cheese. Well-known sheep's cheeses include France's Roquefort and Greece's feta, both of which have been made for hundreds of years. Although sheep,

People have been selectively breeding sheep for centuries, whether for their wool, meat or milk. The eighteenth-century agriculturalist Robert Bakewell revolutionized sheep and cattle breeding in England, with the 'Leicestershire Improved Breed' an example of his work.

Thomas Bewick, illustration to Ralph Beilby's *A General History of Quadrupeds*, 1788–90. UK. Wood engraving on paper. H. 5.2 cm, W. 8.2 cm. 1882,0311.2193. Donated by Isabella Bewick.

Persian fat-tailed sheep naturally store fat in their tails as a source of sustenance. Marco Polo, who visited Persia in the thirteenth century, described sheep with 'long thick tails, weighing thirty pounds and upwards'. The rendered fat is prized in cooking for the richness it provides.

Album leaf, mid-18th century. India. Drawing on paper. H. 43 cm, W. 28.5 cm. 1920,0917,0.99.

being smaller animals, produce less milk than cows, their milk is high in fat and protein and so lends itself to cheese-making. Sheep are fatty animals, and tallow – the rendered fat of sheep – was used for many years to light lamps and to make candles. Over the centuries, hundreds of different breeds of sheep have emerged, some, like Merino sheep, bred for their wool, others for their meat and milk.

Sheep were used as a sacrificial animal in many parts of the world, including ancient Egypt, Greece, Rome and China. The Bible contains many references to ovine sacrifice, and sheep are an important symbolic animal in Christianity. In Islamic tradition, it is customary to mark Eid al-Adha by sacrificing a livestock animal, a sheep, lamb, goat, cow, bull or camel, with the meat then shared with the poor.

Sheep meat is classified by its age, lamb being the meat from young animals, and mutton that from older sheep. Lamb, with its softer texture and more delicate flavour, is the preferred meat in some societies, while tougher, tastier mutton is more popular in others. Tender suckling lambs have long been considered a delicacy, traditionally eaten at Easter in such countries as Greece and Italy.

Right, top: In Roman mythology, it was a shepherd, Faustulus, who discovered the twins Romulus and Remus, who had been suckled by a she-wolf. Faustulus raised the twins as shepherds, and they went on to found Rome. In this Roman silver statuette, a shepherd carries a sheep in a skin bag slung over his shoulder.

Figure, probably 1st century CE. Italy. Silver. H. 8 cm. 1867,0508.764.

Right, bottom: In Christianity, the gentle, caring nature of Jesus Christ is compared to the devotion of shepherds, who tend and protect their sheep from cold, wolves and thieves. This seventeenth-century ivory carving of Christ the Good Shepherd was made by local craftsmen in Goa, India, for the Jesuit missionary market.

Sculpture, early to mid-17th century. Goa, India. Ivory. H. 23.1 cm. 1856,0623.161.

Opposite: These eighteenth-century porcelain figures depict a shepherdess in a simple country dress and apron with a lamb at her feet, and a shepherd with a dog and a ewe. An imaginary pastoral fantasy that romanticizes nature and farm work, the figures bear no resemblance to the harsh, impoverished realities of rural life at the time.

Pair of figures, from Bow Porcelain Factory, *c.* 1765. London, UK. Porcelain, gold. H. 29.4 cm. 1923,1218.1.CR. Bequeathed by Charles Borradaile.

CATTLE

'Cattle' is a collective term used to describe animals in the genus *Bos*, of the family *Bovidae*. Domesticated cattle – notably *Bos taurus*, the European animal, *Bos indicus*, the humped Zebu cattle found in South Asia and Africa, and the water buffalo (*Bubalus bubalis*) – have been important livestock animals in countries around the world for millennia. It is assumed that both *Bos taurus* and *Bos indicus* are descended from the wild aurochs (*Bos primigenius*) that roamed over a large part of the northern hemisphere. There are depictions of these huge, fierce creatures, which had horns up to two metres long, in Palaeolithic cave paintings in Europe. They were hunted for centuries, eventually to extinction, with the last aurochs dying in Poland in 1627. It is thought that cattle became domesticated in three regions, more than 8,000 years ago, later than sheep and goats.

In agrarian societies, cattle were hugely valued as draught animals, as well as providers of milk, meat, hides for leather, and dung, used as fuel and fertilizer. Oxen (castrated bulls) – large, strong and, importantly, docile – played an important role, as they could be harnessed to wooden ploughs and used to work the land. In addition to pulling ploughs, cattle were used to carry loads, pull vehicles, draw water from wells and work mills. Their milk and meat were also important. Over the centuries, cattle breeding saw the creation of breeds specifically for beef or dairy. In many cultures, beef has long been a prestigious meat; beef steak still carries a cachet today.

A scene carved on a twelfth-century draughts piece made of walrus ivory appears to depict a cow suckling a calf. The human use of cow's milk probably began with the domestication of cattle. As well as being drunk, cow's milk is used to make yoghurt, butter and cheese.

Draughts piece, late 12th century. Cologne, Germany. Walrus ivory. Diam. 6 cm. 1892,0801.35. Donated by Sir Augustus Wollaston Franks.

Certain beef dishes have acquired national associations, including the roast beef of England and the American hamburger (made from ground beef).

Cattle are ruminants, with a digestive system that allows them to obtain energy from fibrous plant matter. Cattle-raising methods have varied with different landscapes and environments. In Africa, for example, there is a long-practised pastoralist tradition in which people follow a nomadic, transhumance lifestyle, moving with their cattle from one grazing ground to another on a seasonal basis. Milk from cattle is a staple food, with cattle blood also consumed. In Latin America and North America, one finds the practice of ranching cattle on large areas of land.

Historically, cattle have been perceived as having an intrinsic value, with owning cattle regarded as a source of wealth and prestige. Indeed, in certain languages the words for 'cattle' are etymologically connected with the words for property and riches. Cattle are also animals of great religious significance. In ancient Egypt, the major goddess Hathor was variously depicted in the form of a woman, a cow, or a cow-headed or cow-eared woman. Powerful, virile bulls were revered in many civilizations, including the Minoan culture in Crete. In Hinduism, the cow is sacred, and killing a cow and eating its flesh is forbidden.

The American cowboy, the mounted hand who rounded up and herded cattle, became an iconic figure in American culture, popularized and glamorized in Hollywood films. Rodeos, riding competitions based on a cowboy's daily tasks, such as calf-roping, remain popular forms of entertainment.

Mary Bonner, two cowboys riding bucking horses, 1924. USA. Aquatint on yellow chine collé paper. H. 15 cm, W. 25 cm. 1924,1218.1. Donated by Mary Bonner.

The WILD BULL,
OF THE ANCIENT CALEDONIAN BREED, NOW IN THE PARK AT CHILLINGHAM-CASTLE,
NORTHUMBERLAND. 1789.

Opposite, top: Cylinder-shaped seals were used in the ancient Near East from about 3400 BCE for more than three thousand years. Made generally from stone, they were carved with a design in intaglio so that, when rolled on clay, they left a design in relief. This chalcedony seal shows a humped zebu cow suckling a calf.

Cylinder seal, 6th–4th century BCE. Iraq. Chalcedony. H. 3.35 cm, Diam. 1.6 cm. N.1063.

Opposite, bottom: In this, the largest and most celebrated of his single-sheet engravings, Thomas Bewick depicts the Wild Bull of Chillingham Castle, Northumberland. Bewick captures the formidable power of this long-horned bull, related to the wild cattle known as aurochs from which domestic cattle are also descended.

Thomas Bewick, *The Wild Bull*, 1789. Published in Newcastle upon Tyne, UK. Wood engraving with letterpress on paper. H. 18.5 cm, W. 24 cm. 1871,1209.6468. Donated by W. Carruthers.

Above: As a child, the Hindu deity Krishna was sent away for his safety to be brought up by cowherds. In this painting, Krishna – depicted with blue-black skin, as is traditional – is sitting under a tree with the cowherds, receiving milk from some milkmaids while their cows stand nearby.

Painting, *c.* 1730–40. Painted in the Punjab Hills, India. Gouache on paper. H. 26.9 cm, W. 16.6 cm. 1948,1009,0.114. Bequeathed by Percival Chater Manuk and Gertrude Mary Coles, funded by Art Fund (as NACF).

Below, top: This sketch of two resting goats was drawn by the Persian artist Janí, who called himself 'Farangi Saz', meaning 'painter in the European style'. He was working in Isfahan for the German naturalist, physician and explorer Dr Engelbert Kaempfer, who was living in Persia at the time.

Painting, from *Album of Persian Costumes and Animals with Some Drawings by Kaempfer*, drawn by Janí, 1684–85. Isfahan, Iran. Ink and watercolour on paper. H. 21.4 cm, W. 29.9 cm. 1974,0617,0.1.22. Bequeathed by Sir Hans Sloane.

Below, bottom: In the ancient Greek and Roman worlds, the ritual sacrifice of such domestic animals as oxen, goats and sheep was a central act of worship. The chosen animals might be garlanded with flowers or ribbons before being sacrificed within the sanctuary; the entrails and meat of the sacrificed animal were then consumed by the worshippers.

Lamp filler, 1st century BC. Made in Campania, Italy, excavated in Rhodes, Greece. Terracotta. H. 10.16 cm, L. 10.16 cm. 1873,0820.590.

Opposite: This Neo-Assyrian figure, a man with large wings, is a protective spirit, most likely an *apkallu*. The kilt with long tassels he is wearing is a sign of his semi-divine status. In his hands he carries a goat and a giant ear of grain. These objects might be symbolic of fertility, although their exact meaning is unknown.

Relief wall panel, 875–860 BCE. Nimrud, Iraq. Gypsum. H. 224 cm, W. 127 cm, D. 12 cm. 1849,0502.2.

POULTRY

Of the various domesticated birds kept for their meat and eggs, it is the chicken that is best known and widely reared and consumed. The domestic chicken (*Gallus domesticus*) is descended from the jungle fowl *Gallus gallus*, a bird native to the Indian subcontinent and Southeast Asia. When and where the chicken was first domesticated is uncertain, but Southeast Asia is considered likely. The chicken is thought to have spread from there into Egypt and then into Europe. Chicken breeding became a craze in Europe and North America during the nineteenth century, triggered by the gift to Queen Victoria of large, strikingly colourful birds from China known as Cochin chickens. At one time chicken meat was a luxury; today, however, intensively produced chicken, from birds bred to grow fast and slaughtered at a few weeks of age, is cheap and widely available.

In addition to being valued for their meat, chickens are prized for their prolific egg-laying capabilities; indeed, they may well have been domesticated for this purpose. Historically, the egg has been considered a symbol of life and appears in many creation myths. A hen's egg is an excellent source of high-quality protein, as well as iron, trace minerals and various vitamins. In the kitchen, the protein content in eggs makes them noticeably versatile foodstuffs that can be cooked in numerous ways: boiled, fried, baked, steamed and scrambled. Egg yolks are used to enrich cakes, pastry and custards, while egg whites, with their capacity to be whisked, are appreciated for the lightness they offer in the form of meringues or sponges.

This portrait of a trader carefully holding a large tray of eggs dates from the Qajar period in Iran (1779–1924). There are a number of classic egg dishes in Persian cuisine, including *kuku sabzi* (herb omelette), *khagineh* (sweet omelette) and *mirza qasemi* (aubergine, tomatoes and eggs).

Drawing of an egg seller, c. 1850. Iran. Watercolour on paper. H. 15.4 cm, W. 11.1 cm. 2006,0314,0.16.

Before one can cook such birds as chickens, their feathers have to be removed from their carcasses. Historically, this slow and messy operation was best done outdoors. Here, a Parisian fireman is making advances to a poultry-seller, busy at work plucking a chicken in her lap.

Nicolas Toussaint Charlet, a Parisian fireman in a market, 1824–87. Published in Paris, France. Lithograph on paper. H. 35.6 cm, W. 27 cm. 1869,0410.64.

Other domesticated birds include ducks, geese and turkeys. The domestic duck is descended from the wild mallard (*Anas platyrhynchos*), with Southeast Asia considered a major centre of domestication. Ducks are an important bird in this part of the world, prized for their capacity to forage in paddy fields and control pests, as well as for their rich meat and eggs. Domestic geese are descended from two species of wild geese: the greylag (*Anser anser*) and the swan goose (*Anser cygnoides*). There are records of domesticated geese in ancient Egypt, and they became popular in Europe during Roman times. Geese have long been enjoyed for their rich, flavourful meat, with their ample fat providing a quality ingredient in cooking. The domestic turkey has its origins in two wild turkeys found in the Americas: the ocellated turkey (*Meleagris ocellata*) and the wild turkey (*Meleagris gallopavo*), which were domesticated by Indigenous peoples. Spanish colonialists encountered turkeys in the New World and introduced them to Europe in the early 1500s. There, these large birds were readily accepted, with their size lending themselves to celebratory feasting. Today, the turkey is a staple of Thanksgiving meals in North America and is eaten at Christmas in such countries as Britain.

Above: Dating from the Ming dynasty, this porcelain wine cup is known as a 'chicken cup', after the subject of the design on its exterior. Such cups were decorated using the doucai technique, a complex, intricate method in which layers of coloured enamels are painted over an outline design to evoke different textures – in this case, the cockerel's feathers and the hen's wings.

Wine cup, 1465–87. Jingdezhen, China. Glazed porcelain. H. 3.8 cm, Diam. 8.3 cm. PDF,A.748. On loan to the British Museum from the Sir Percival David Collection.

Below: This painting of a chicken by Noda Tomin was copied from another artist's copies of 'Sketches of Various Birds' by the master Kano Tan'yu. Artists of the influential Kano school trained by copying the work of earlier masters of the school.

Noda Tomin, a chicken, 1792. Japan. Ink and colour painting on paper. H. 28.1 cm, W. 40.7 cm. 1881,1210,0.2451.

Domestic chickens were valued for various reasons in Roman times, including for cockfighting. Columella, the Roman author of *De re rustica* (On Agriculture), gave detailed instructions on their breeding, keeping and fattening. *De re coquinaria* (The Art of Cooking), the cookbook credited to the Roman gourmet Apicius, includes recipes for chicken.

Mosaic, 4th century. Halicarnassus, Turkey. Stone. W. 43.5 cm.
1857,1220.425

THE PIG

The domestic pig (*Sus scrofa domesticus*) is descended from the wild boar (*Sus scrofa*). Wild boars are omnivorous and inquisitive, traits that are presumed to have been factors in their domestication in around the eighth millennium BCE. Archaeological evidence points to both China and the Middle East as places where domestication took place. The natural habitat of wild boars is woodland, but it is thought that the animals were attracted to the rubbish heaps and crops of early farming settlements and so began living in proximity to humans. Captured wild-boar piglets could be easily tamed and then used for breeding – a process that led eventually to the domestic pig.

Pigs are kept for their meat. Qualities that led to their popularity as livestock animals include their ability to forage successfully for their own food and to thrive on scraps. From a physiological point of view, pigs are well equipped as foragers, possessing sharp teeth, which allow them to eat a variety of foods; an impressive sense of smell; and a snout tough enough to enable them to dig into the ground and rootle out edible tubers. That pigs are prolific – with sows having litters of around ten piglets – and that the animals gain weight quickly, so offering a substantial carcass when killed, were additional factors in making them valued meat animals.

Pigs are an important source of meat in many parts of the world, from Denmark to Polynesia. Sailors were able to successfully transport pigs on sea voyages, which saw them spread around the world. Christopher Columbus brought pigs to the New World in 1493; from an original eight pigs left on the island of Hispaniola, the population multiplied and became feral. In China, the pig is regarded as such an important animal that the Chinese character for 'home' consists of a pig under a roof; in addition, the word for 'meat' automatically means pork, unless otherwise specified.

Pork was a popular meat in ancient Rome. Pigs were also adorned and sacrificed to the gods. The *suovetaurilia* was a form of Roman animal sacrifice in which three animals – a pig (*sus*), a sheep (*ovis*) and a bull (*taurus*) – were killed together, giving the ritual its name.

Figure, 1st century BCE – 1st century CE. Rome, Italy. Bronze. H. 2.54 cm. 1824,0414.1. Bequeathed by Richard Payne Knight.

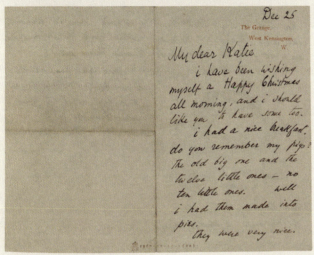

This whimsical, illustrated letter – one of a series sent by the artist Edward Burne-Jones to Katie Lewis, daughter of the solicitor Sir George Lewis – sums up the common fate suffered by pigs: 'i had a nice breakfast. do you remember my pigs? The old big one and the / twelve little ones – no / ten little ones. well / I had them made into / pies. / they were very nice.'

Edward Burne-Jones, letter from *Letters to Katie*, 1883–89. UK. Pen and brown ink drawing on paper. H. 17.5 cm, W. 22.5 cm. 1960,1014.2.20. Bequeathed by Katherine Lewis.

Historically, because pigs can be fed on waste and housed in confined spaces, keeping a pig was a viable option for poorer households. The practice of annually keeping a pig then slaughtering it for its meat was commonplace. In China, rural households continue to rear pigs in preparation for Chinese New Year feasting, as has been done for centuries. In Europe, the killing of a household pig in the cold winter months is also a long-held custom; depicted in fifteenth- and sixteenth-century books of hours, it still takes place in some parts of the continent.

The abundance of meat on a pig carcass, combined with the importance for many of not wasting any part of it, has seen pork preserved in numerous ways. Pork is the key meat in both European and Chinese charcuterie, ingeniously transformed into bacon, sausages, salamis and hams. Lard, the fat from pigs, is a useful ingredient, prized by cooks, bakers and charcutiers alike.

Pork as a meat is taboo in some religions, notably Judaism and Islam. The fact that pigs are undiscriminating eaters, known to feed on rubbish, dead meat and excrement – the very trait that made pigs so valued as livestock animals – meant that they were considered unclean, and the consumption of their meat was forbidden. Overall, however, pork is a widely eaten meat, second only to chicken in popularity.

According to Chinese legend, Emperor Yao, searching for a worthy successor, was told of a filial young man called Shun at Mount Li. Shun inspired such devotion that elephants and birds came to help him plough his family's fields. Indeed, so impressive was Shun that Emperor Yao appointed him his successor.

Wang Xin, *Shun Ploughing at Mount Li*, c. 1690–1720. Suzhou, China. Woodblock print on paper. H. 29 cm, W. 29 cm. 1928,0323,0.29. Bequeathed by Sir Hans Sloane.

While this bronze statuette shows a scene that was common in Roman rural life, the bull and the cow depicted would have made an impractical ploughing team. This suggests that the piece may instead refer to the generation of new life or the setting out of new city boundaries, when a furrow was indeed ploughed by such a team, to bring good luck.

Figure, 1st–3rd century CE. Piercebridge, UK. Copper alloy. H. 4.5 cm, L. 7.1 cm. 1879,0710.1. Donated by Sir Augustus Wollaston Franks.

Right: This Chinese wooden yoke has been inlaid with representations of auspicious objects from both the natural and the man-made world: bats, fish, Chinese knots, *ruyi* (a fungus said to confer immortality), coins and the *wan* symbol. Such representations might have had a protective purpose – in this instance, to protect a beast of burden from malign forces.

Yoke, 19th century. Chinese communities, Thailand. Wood, white metal. H. 20.5 cm, W. 21 cm, D. 2.5 cm. As1910,-.40. Donated by H. B. Garrett.

Below: Water buffalo have long been important draught animals in Asia. As their name suggests, they thrive in watery environments, such as swamps. In southern China and Southeast Asia, the water buffalo is particularly valued for its ability to plough wet rice fields.

Banknote, 1958. Issued in Cambodia. Paper. H. 9.9 cm, W. 18.2 cm. 2007,4156.3. Donated by Daniel Alberman.

Travel and trade

Food has a striking capacity to travel. Many ingredients now regarded as typical of national cuisines originated in countries far away. As people moved from one place to another, dishes, cooking methods and foodstuffs moved with them, fanning out across the globe. Market forces were also involved: historic trade routes over land and sea saw livestock, plants and ingredients transported long distances to satisfy demand.

Over the millennia, empires have played a major role in spreading foodstuffs around the world. The Roman Empire is credited with introducing items including grape vines and apples to the lands it had conquered; citizens in Rome ate a diet rich in foods imported from the provinces. Among the factors that led such European maritime nations as Portugal, the Netherlands and Britain to establish colonies overseas was the desire to find the sources of valuable spices and create trade monopolies.

The phrase 'Columbian Exchange' (after the Italian explorer Christopher Columbus), or 'Grand Exchange', refers to the transfer of populations, diseases, ideas, commodities and foods between the Americas and Afro-Eurasia after Columbus's first voyage to the New World in 1492 and the subsequent colonization of the region by European powers. The consequences of the Columbian Exchange were huge and complex, shaping societies, agriculture and cuisines worldwide. Staple crops were part of this exchange; these foods expanded people's diets and were an important source of calories, enabling and supporting population growth.

The Spanish colonialists are credited with introducing various domestic animals to the New World: horses, cattle, sheep, goats and pigs. Two major grain crops were also introduced to the Americas by European settlers: rice and wheat. Over the centuries, the Great Plains of North America were ploughed and planted, and today the United States is a major producer of wheat. Among the foodstuffs that Columbus brought to the New World was sugar cane, in 1493. The European demand for sugar – and the hard physical labour required to grow and harvest sugar cane and process its juice into sugar – was central to the Transatlantic slave trade.

Several foodstuffs were taken in the opposite direction, from the New World to the Old World. Among them were cacao, the tomato and two important staples: maize from Mesoamerica and the potato from Peru. Once the potato plant had adapted to European growing conditions – notably the variations in daylight hours – its value as a calorific and prolific food crop was recognized and it was widely adopted as such. The chilli, now considered a characteristic part of Indian, Korean and Southeast Asian cooking, is yet another New World ingredient that has spread around the planet.

Today, in an age of air travel and temperature-controlled supply chains, we live in a globalized food system in which foodstuffs, from staples to luxuries, are moved around the world to an extraordinary extent.

Left, top: Pacific Islanders are some of the most skilled voyagers to have travelled the world's oceans. On their canoes, they carried with them seedlings and plants to cultivate when they reached new lands. This navigation chart served as a memory aide for Islanders learning to read the ocean. The shells represent islands, while the curved sticks represent the swell and how it moves between island groups.

Navigation chart, 19th century. Marshall Islands. Palm leaf, bast, shell. H. 26.3 cm, W. 72.5 cm, D. 2.5 cm. Oc1944,02.931. Donated by Irene Marguerite Beasley.

Left, bottom: Trade in food, raw materials and objects has been taking place for millennia. The practice of following defined routes based on observations of the night sky, thereby making journeys easier, developed in the Arab world and spread to Europe. This astrolabe, made in England in the Middle Ages, demonstrates a knowledge of Arabic astronomy and instrumentation.

Astrolabe, 1290–1300. UK. Copper alloy, brass (?). Diam. 46.2 cm, D. 1.2 cm. SLMathInstr.54. Bequeathed by Sir Hans Sloane.

Above: The Perry Scroll depicts a key event in Japanese history. In 1853, in a challenge to Japan's self-imposed restrictions on relations with the outside world, in place since the late 1630s, US Commodore Matthew Perry brought warships into Edo Bay and demanded the establishment of trade relations between America and Japan. A trade treaty was signed the following year.

Hibata Ōsuke, Takagawa Bunsen and Onuma Chinzan, *The Mission of Commodore Perry to Japan in 1854*, 1854–58. Japan. Painting on silk handscroll. H. 28.9 cm, W. 1525 cm. 2013,3002.1. Purchase funded by the Brooke Sewell Bequest, JTI Japanese Acquisition Fund, Friends of the British Museum, Noriko & Shigeru Myojin, Dounia & Sherif Nadar, Adeela Qureshi, Richard de Unger and Mitsubishi Corporation.

Below: Cloves from the Moluccas, a group of islands in Indonesia also known as Maluku and formerly called the Spice Islands, were much sought after by Europeans and were at the heart of the spice trade from the 1500s. This miniature boat, made from tightly packed cloves, is thought to be a *kora kora* – a long, narrow vessel with storage for trade goods that was also used for warfare.

Model boat, late 18th – early 20th century. Maluku, Indonesia. Clove, fibre. H. 30 cm, D. 23 cm, L. 58 cm. As1972,Q.1944.

SUGAR

Sweetness in food and drink has long been prized by humans, and sugar (sucrose) is the world's most important sweetener. We enjoy its flavour and value it for the energy it gives us, as a concentrated form of calories. Once a luxury, reserved for consumption by the elite, it is now generally available and affordable, widely used in commercial food manufacturing as well as in domestic kitchens.

For much of its history, sugar was made from the juice of the sugar cane (*Saccharum officinarum*), a grass that grows in the tropics, thought to have originated in New Guinea and been taken by seafarers to Asia. Crystalline sugar is made by extracting sugar-cane juice and boiling it down until it crystallizes. Sanskrit texts suggest that this process was known in north India around 500 BCE. Both sugar cane and the technique for making sugar gradually spread to the Mediterranean region, a journey in which the Arab world played a significant part – Venice being an important hub for the Arab sugar trade with Europe. Sugar was initially a costly, exotic ingredient, valued for its medicinal properties as well as for its sweetness. It was also appreciated for its preserving qualities, used for centuries to create candied peels and glacé fruits.

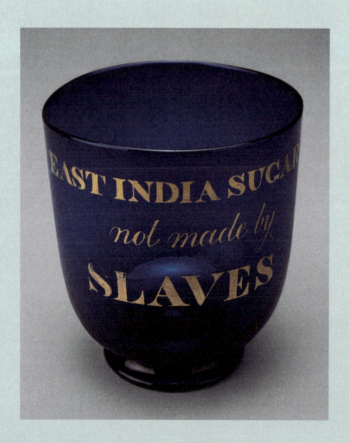

Sugar production in the colonized West Indies was based on the enslavement of Africans. Campaigners for the abolition of the slave trade looked for other ethical sugar sources and promoted the cause in their tea sets. This glass bowl is unusual, as most abolitionist bowls from the 1820s are made from porcelain.

Sugar bowl, c. 1820–30. Bristol (?), UK. Glass, wood, brass, gold. H. 11 cm, Diam. 10 cm. 2002,0904.1.

This intricately worked silver sugar basin was made in the workshop of Oomersee Mawjee, a renowned Indian silversmith. His customers included British Army personnel, anglophile Indians and Liberty's of London. The foliage decorating the basin contains birds and animals, while the lid has a knob in the form of a crouching tiger.

Sugar basin, late 19th century. Workshop of Oomersee Mawjee, Bhuj, India. Silver. H. 16.5 cm, W. 15.2 cm, D. 10.7 cm. 2011,3014.47. Bequeathed by Oppi Untracht.

It was during the eighteenth century that European sugar consumption increased considerably. This increase was directly connected to slavery and the establishment by European colonial powers of plantations in the Americas, where sugar cane was grown and processed into crystalline sugar. Production took place on or near sugar-cane plantations in the tropics, as the sugar cane needed to be processed as soon as possible after harvest. The triangular Transatlantic slave trade saw manufactured goods taken from Britain to Africa, where they were traded for enslaved people; these people were then transported to the Americas, where they were used to process the sugar cane into crystalline sugar; finally, the processed sugar was taken to Britain for domestic consumption and export. Sugar became far more affordable and widely consumed, in drinks including tea and coffee and in such foods as jam. During the nineteenth century, the resistance of enslaved people and the Abolitionist movement succeeded in bringing about the end of slavery.

The nineteenth century also saw the arrival of a temperate, plant-based alternative to cane sugar, namely beet sugar. In 1747, a Prussian chemist named Andreas Marggraf demonstrated that he could produce sugar crystals from the juice of white beet (*Beta vulgaris*) that were chemically identical to those derived from sugar cane. His discovery paved the way for the rise of the sugar-beet industry in Europe.

For centuries, sugar was produced in the form of solid, cone-shaped blocks, known as sugar loaves. In 1875, Henry Tate bought the rights to an invention that could cut up sugar loaves into small cubes. Today, industrial sugar production carefully controls the crystallization process to create the small, uniformly sized sugar crystals we have become familiar with.

Valued for their ability to carry heavy loads in all weathers, caravans of both Bactrian and dromedary camels were used to move bulky goods along the trade routes between the Middle East and Central and South Asia – the pre-modern equivalent of lorries or container ships. Camels were useful in several other ways too: their hair could be be spun and woven into cloth, while their milk and meat were valued as food.

Painting, c. 1600. Iran. Ink, watercolour and gold on paper. H. 30.4 cm, W. 20.4 cm. 1922,1017,0.2.

A *famille rose* plate marking the anchorage of a Dutch East Indiamen, the *Vrijburg*, in Chinese waters in the 1750s. Voyages to China from the Dutch East India company base at Batavia in Indonesia could only be undertaken once a year because of the prevailing tides and weather conditions.

Plate, 1756. Jingdezhen, Jiangxi province, China. Glazed porcelain. H. 2.5 cm, Diam. 22.8 cm. Franks.598. Donated by Sir Augustus Wollaston Franks.

Models such as this one are among the few remaining traces of the merchant sailing vessels, known locally as *yathra dhoni*, that were once used to transport cargo between India and Sri Lanka. According to reports, the last of these boats was wrecked in the Maldives in the 1930s.

Boat model, 19th century. Sri Lanka or India. Wood, textile. H. 10 cm, W. 40.7 cm, D. 35.9 cm. As1933,1110.1. Donated by Royal Artillery Institute.

CHOCOLATE

For much of its long history, chocolate was consumed as a liquid, rather than as a solid food. Chocolate, both the beverage and the eating variety, is made from the seeds – known as beans – of the tropical cacao plant (*Theobroma cacao*). Exactly where *Theobroma cacao* originated from is much disputed, with the Amazon region one possibility. What is not contested, however, is that the first recorded histories of cacao can be found in Mesoamerica. The cacao plant and its edible beans were hugely important in the region, both culturally and economically, featuring in Mesoamerica's ancient mythologies. Chocolate was drunk at ceremonies and rituals, and elaborate vessels for the drinking of chocolate were buried in the tombs of Maya elite. Cacao beans also had an intrinsic value, and were used as currency and tribute. Drinking chocolate was made by grinding cacao nibs and mixing them with water. The creation of a foam by pouring the liquid from one container to another was an important feature of the drink's preparation. The beverage was also flavoured in various ways, including with vanilla and chilli.

Christopher Columbus encountered cacao on a voyage in 1502, when he captured a Maya trading canoe with cacao beans in its hold. The Spanish, who invaded Mexico in 1519–21 under the conquistador Hernando Cortés, are credited with introducing chocolate to Europe. Initially, this novel beverage was an exotic luxury, drunk by members of European royalty and aristocracy in the courts. Gradually, however, the drink's popularity spread,

The Mixtec culture is one of the important pre-colonial cultures of Mesoamerica. In this iconic scene from the Tonindeye Codex, Lady Thirteen Serpent 'Cocoa Flower' offers a tripod vessel full of chocolate to the Mixtec ruler Lord Eight Deer 'Jaguar Claw' during their marriage ceremony in 1104 CE.

Codex, 1200–1521. La Mixteca, Mexico. Deer skin, plaster, chalk, natural pigments. H. 19 cm, W. 23.5 cm (page). Am1902,0308.1. Donated by Ms Curzon.

with chocolate-houses – for the drinking of chocolate – opening in Paris and London during the seventeenth century.

It was during the Industrial Revolution that chocolate was transformed from a beverage into the solid form we know it by today. The manufacture of chocolate is a long, complex process. Cacao pods are harvested from cacao trees; the cacao beans are then separated from the pulp, fermented and dried. Often, these dried, fermented beans are then transported from their country of origin to other countries to be turned into chocolate. To make chocolate, the cacao beans are first roasted and then ground, before being further processed. The invention of certain pieces of machinery was key to the industrialization and wide-scale production of chocolate. In 1828, Coenraad van Houten, a Dutch inventor, unveiled a machine that pressed out the natural fat from cacao beans, separating cocoa solids from cocoa butter. In 1847, Joseph Fry started selling the world's first chocolate bars, made by mixing a proportion of cocoa butter with cocoa solids. In 1878, a Swiss manufacturer by the name of Rodolphe Lindt invented the conche machine, which, by slowly turning and aerating cocoa mass, greatly improved eating chocolate's texture. Eating chocolate became a popular ingredient in the manufacture of confectionary and patisserie.

Cacao is grown in the tropics, in an area ranging from 20 degrees north to 20 degrees south of the equator; today, West Africa produces more than two-thirds of the world's cacao. Mass-produced chocolate is widely available, while recent years have seen the rise of a craft chocolate movement in various countries. Regardless of its credentials, chocolate continues to enjoy a reputation as an indulgent treat.

Above, left: This lidded Maya pottery vessel is decorated with eleven figures, thought to be girls taking part in a sacrificial dance. It also features a glyph for cacao – *kakaw* in Maya. The word 'cacao' is a Hispanicization of the name given to the plant in indigenous Mesoamerican languages.

Vessel, Classic Maya (250–900 CE). Guatemala. Pottery. H. 25 cm, W. 18 cm, D. 18.2 cm. Am1974,08.1.a.

Above, right: As European trade with the West Indies increased during the seventeenth century, so did the popularity of drinking chocolate, made from imported cacao beans. So fashionable was this exotic beverage that dainty cups made in gold, silver or porcelain were produced specially for its consumption.

Pair of cups, made by John Chartier, c. 1700. London, UK. Gold. H. 6.5 cm, Diam 5.9 cm. 2005,0604.1.

La juste Épicière.
(Paris.)

Published by Charles Tilt, 86 fleet street London.

Opposite: Concerns over the accuracy of scales and dishonest merchants' dubious weighing practices have long existed. This anxiety is alluded to in the title of this French print, *La Juste Epicière* (The Fair Grocer), which shows a young woman carefully – and presumably scrupulously – weighing goods on a set of scales.

Charles Philipon, *La Juste Epicière* (The Fair Grocer), 1824. Published in Paris, France. Hand-coloured lithograph on paper. H. 24.6 cm, W. 15.8 cm. 1948,0217.78. Donated by Raymond Willis.

Above: Metal market weights were used by Burmese traders as counterbalances on hand-held scales, which consisted of trays suspended from either end of a rod. The weights came in sets of up to ten, often in the form of Burma's sacred birds, the *hintha* – as seen here – or the *karaweik*.

Weights, 1800–1860. Burma. Brass or bronze. Largest H. 12 cm, W. 7 cm, D. 5.5 cm. As.5866.a-g. Exchanged with Royal United Service Institution (United Service Museum) in 1869.

Below: Between 2600 and 1900 BCE, the Indus civilization was a network of cities in the northwestern part of the Indian subcontinent with thriving trade links to the world beyond. This seal, found in the Indus Valley itself, was used to stamp clay sealings on ropes wrapped around bundles of goods.

Stamp seal, 2600–1900 BCE. Harappa, Pakistan. Steatite. H. 2.4 cm, W. 2.5 cm, D. 1.4 cm. 1892,1210.1. Donated by Maj. Gen. Malcolm George Clerk.

TRAVEL, TRADE AND EMPIRE · QUALITY CONTROL

SPICES

For centuries, spices were seen as highly valuable and were much sought after. The history of spices is intertwined with trade, colonization, migration and monopolies. The term 'spices' is used to describe a group of plant-based flavourings – consisting of seeds, bark, roots, rhizomes, stigmas – that are usually, but not always, dried. Historically, spices have been prized for their fragrance and their medicinal, culinary and preserving properties.

Small, light, portable and, significantly, perceived as precious, spices were ideal commodities for trading. Spices have been traded for thousands of years, with trade routes established around the world, over both land and sea. Many of the spices particularly prized in Europe – pepper, cinnamon, cloves, nutmeg and ginger – come from the Asian tropics. By the time these spices reached Europe, they had been on long, demanding and dangerous journeys, and had passed through many hands. As a consequence, they were given a high price tag. Italian city-states, such as strategically positioned Venice, profited hugely from the spice trade. In European countries, where imported spices were an expensive luxury, using large quantities of them in the kitchen signalled affluence and was a trademark of courtly cuisine.

The desire to find the Far Eastern sources of these spices and establish their own, lucrative trade routes was a motivating factor for European maritime powers in the fifteenth and sixteenth centuries, leading to colonialism and empire-building around the world. Take, for example, the story of nutmeg. The nutmeg tree (*Myristica fragrans*) is native to the Moluccas, an island archipelago in Indonesia also known as the Spice Islands. When the Portuguese

By the first millennium BCE, trade in pepper (*Piper nigrum*), which is native to the southwest coast of India, had reached the Middle East and Europe. This opulent, silver-gilt pepper pot, known as the Hoxne 'Empress' pepper pot after the hoard in which it was found, shows that the spice was a valued commodity.

Pepper pot, 300–400 CE. Hoxne, UK. Silver, gold. H. 10.3 cm, W. 5.7 cm. 1994,0408.33. HM Treasury Treasure Trove, purchase funded with contribution from Art Fund (as NACF), National Heritage Memorial Fund and British Museum Friends (as British Museum Society).

Left, top: The chilli pepper, as depicted here on a Nazca pottery bowl, has long been cultivated in the Americas. European colonizers and traders introduced the spice to Europe, and played a key role in spreading it to Africa, India and Southeast Asia.

Bowl, 100 BCE–600 CE. Nazca Valley, Peru. Pottery. H. 8.5 cm, W. 20.5 cm, D. 20.5 cm. Am1912,0717.34.

Left, bottom: Nutmeg imported from the East Indies was so highly prized in Britain that luxury goods were produced to show the spice off. Made in the early eighteenth century, this engraved silver box features two hinged compartments, a central space for a nutmeg grater, and ducal coronets emblazoned on either side.

Nutmeg grater and box, made by David Tanqueray, 1715. London, UK. Silver. H. 7 cm, W. 8 cm, D. 12 cm. 1969,0705.33. Bequeathed by Peter Wilding.

reached the Moluccas in 1514, they established a monopoly in the nutmeg trade that lasted for almost a century. After the Dutch had taken control of the islands from the Portuguese in the early part of the seventeenth century, they retained their monopoly on nutmeg for 150 years. In a bid to break this monopoly, the French succeeded in cultivating imported nutmeg seedlings on Mauritius. During the nineteenth century, the British introduced nutmeg plants to the Caribbean, establishing it successfully on the island of Grenada. To this day, Grenada remains a major producer of nutmeg.

When it comes to cooking, spices are notably versatile ingredients, able to be used in both savoury and sweet dishes. Furthermore, spices can be blended together to create new flavour combinations. Cuisines around the world – such as Indian, Mexican and Malaysian – have developed their own, distinctive spice repertoires and ways of cooking with them. These range from creating spice pastes from powdered spices to adding them whole to rice dishes or stews to imbue them with their fragrance. The most expensive spice today is saffron, owing to the intensive labour involved in harvesting it. Made from the dried stigmas of the saffron crocus (*Crocus sativa*), around 70,000 flowers are required in order to produce 450 grams of the spice.

Glazed pottery was one of many products made in and traded from the historic Iraqi port of Basra. Inspired by Chinese porcelain imports shipped from China in *dhows*, this jar is decorated with splashed glaze in blue and green over a pale body.

Jar, 9th century. Found in Iran. Glazed pottery. H. 24 cm, Diam. 28.3 cm. 1930,0310.1.

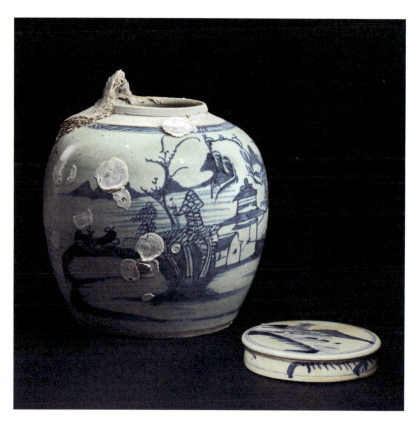

This blue-and-white porcelain ginger jar, with seashells attached from its time spent below the waves, was recovered from the wreck of *The Diana*, a merchant ship of the Honourable East India Company, which sank in the Strait of Malacca on 4 March 1817. The ship was carrying 24,000 pieces of Chinese porcelain, along with tea and spices.

Ginger jar, 1816. Made in Jingdezhen, China, found off the coast of Malacca, Malaysia. Glazed porcelain. H. 22 cm, Diam. 12 cm. 1995,0619.1.a-b. Purchased from Heirloom and Howard Ltd, funded by Brooke Sewell Permanent Fund.

For thousands of years, sizeable pottery vessels known as amphorae were used for the storage and transportation of food and drink. The ancient Greeks and Romans kept wine and olive oil in such vessels, as well as meat, fish and dry goods. This transport 'bobbin' amphora was made on the island of Chios, noted for its wine.

Amphora, 600–550 BCE. Made in Chios, Greece, excavated in Naukratis, Egypt. Pottery. H. 68 cm, Diam. 29.2 cm. 2006,0331.18.

Religion

Food plays a part in religion in different ways. In many cultures, food is used as a means of interacting with the gods and spirits and gaining their favour. The practice of making offerings of food to deities, or to the ancestors who mediate with the heavens on behalf of the living, is found in religions around the world. These food offerings take various forms. The ritual sacrifice of living animals to the gods was a feature of religious life in many societies, including the Incas, the ancient Egyptians, the Mesopotamians and the Chinese. In ancient Greece and Rome, meat from the sacrificial animals was burnt, with the scent of the smoke rising from it thought to please the gods.

Food and religion are also linked by the rules in some belief systems regarding which foods may or may not be eaten. In ancient Egypt, certain species of Nile fish had religious associations and so their consumption was forbidden. The dietary laws of kashrut are an important part of Judaism, and were observed by all Jews universally until the late eighteenth century. The laws are based on the Torah, which contains the divine commandments revealed by God to Moses, and the Talmud, comprising ancient, sacred teachings. The kashrut spell out what is permitted within the laws (*kosher*) and what is forbidden (*terefah*). Pork is one of the forbidden foods within Judaism. The eating of blood is also prohibited, so there are strict rules regarding the handling of meat, from ritual slaughter and butchering to preparation and cooking. Cooking is forbidden during the Jewish Sabbath, with food prepared in advance. Cholent, a typical Sabbath meat stew, is made on a Friday and left to cook overnight in a very low oven. In Islam, the rules regarding dietary prohibitions are recorded in the Quran and the Hadith. The divine word of God revealed to the Prophet Muhammad divides food into the permitted (*halal*) and the forbidden (*haram*). Among the forbidden foods and drinks are pork and alcohol. Blood is also forbidden, and animals are slaughtered according to prescribed methods laid down in Islamic law. Many Hindus and Buddhists follow vegetarian diets, and vegetarianism is practised by followers of Jainism, an Indian religion centred on a belief in *ahimsa* (non-violence).

Many religious calendars are marked by prescribed periods of fasting – requiring abstinence from specific foods – and feasting, with certain foods eaten as part of a celebration. Religious festivals are often associated with particular dishes and foodstuffs. These celebratory foods can have symbolic meanings attached to them, as in the case of *lampropsomo*, the Greek Easter bread decorated with red-dyed, hard-boiled eggs, which symbolize both the blood of Christ and his rebirth.

This section of the frieze from the Parthenon shows a group of youths taking part in the Panathenaic festival (held to celebrate the birthday of the goddess Athena), leading a cow to be sacrificed. The animal strains its neck upwards in protest. It is thought that this scene inspired the poet John Keats to write of 'the heifer lowing to the skies' in his poem 'Ode on a Grecian Urn'.

Relief, 438–432 BCE. Athens, Greece. Marble. H. 1.02 m.
1816,0610.86.

Left: In this scene on the side of a Greek amphora, two bulls are being prepared for sacrifice in a sanctuary dedicated to Dionysus. The sacrificial animals are being adorned with *stemmata*, or woollen sacrificial fillets, which marked the animals out as sacred to the deity.

Amphora, c. 450 BCE. Made in Athens, Greece. Pottery. H. 44.5 cm. 1846,0128.1.

Below: This brass gold-weight, used to weigh out measures of gold dust in West Africa, shows a man sacrificing a fowl as part of a ritual known as the *Kyekyere Nkabere* charm. This ritual was performed throughout the Asante region of West Africa during the pre-colonial and early colonial era.

Gold-weight, 18th–20th century. Made by Akan people, Ghana. Brass. H. 3 cm, W. 1.75 cm, D. 4 cm. Af1954,23.2147. Donated by Wellcome Institute for the History of Medicine.

The annual Annakuta Festival in Nathdwara, northwest India, is observed by donating a mound of rice to the temple of Srinathji to honour the moment when Krishna lifted Mount Govardhan to protect his villagers. During the festival, the temple is filled with food offerings, depicted here alongside the pile of rice symbolizing the mountain.

Painting, late 18th century. Painted in Nathdwara, India. Gouache on paper. H. 31.5 cm, W. 21.1 cm. 1940,0713,0.67. Donated by Mrs A. G. Moor.

Left, top: This painting depicts a Korean ancestral shrine. While some families had ancestral shrines of their own, shrine paintings were used as a substitute by those who did not or who needed to hold a ritual while away from home. In the foreground, as in actual rituals, a sacrificial table is adorned with fruits, foods, candles and incense.

Painting, 19th century. Korea. Ink and mineral colour on paper. H. 104.5 cm, W. 68 cm. 2010,3024.1. Purchase funded by Hahn Kwang-Ho Purchase Fund.

Left, bottom: *Ding* vessels were ancient Chinese cooking pots reserved for offerings of food to ancestors. Cast in bronze and composed of a round body supported by three legs, the vessels were used throughout the Shang, Zhou, Qin and Han periods (from around 1500 BCE to 220 CE).

Ding vessel, 12th–11th century BCE. China. Bronze. H. 20.3 cm, Diam. 15.9 cm. 1954,0511.1. Donated by P. T. Brooke Sewell.

Below: In Buddhist societies, making offerings to the monkhood is an important duty for lay Buddhists (see also page 133). In Burma, in a practice that dates back several hundred years, food is carried to temples in special offering vessels known as *hsun ok*. The spired lid on this highly elaborate example has a sacred *hintha* bird set into it.

Hsun ok offering vessel, mid- to late 19th century. Mandalay, Burma. Bamboo, lacquer, glass, wood, gold, metal. H. 119 cm, Diam. 56 cm. 1994,1116.2. Acquired by Herbert Allcroft in Burma in 1894–95; sold by the family in 1994; acquired by the museum from Spink & Son Ltd in 1994, funded by Brooke Sewell Permanent Fund.

FOOD FOR THE DEAD

The idea of providing food for the dead to sustain them in the afterlife is found in a number of societies, both past and present.

In ancient Egypt, it was widely believed that in order to experience the afterlife, certain conditions regarding the dead had to be met: the body had to remain intact, the name must carry on, and the spirit of the deceased needed to be given provisions at regular intervals. From the Predynastic Period, burials included personal possessions and pottery containing food and drink. In the Old Kingdom, tombs consisted of the burial place and a funerary chapel, where offerings were presented to nourish and support the dead. Mud-brick tombs sometimes featured stone panels with a carved relief depicting the tomb-owner seated before a table holding food offerings. Over time, funerary chapels – initially simple, mud-brick-walled rooms – developed and became more elaborate. The wealthy were provided with funerary chapels decorated with scenes designed to secure the provision of food and drink. Middle Kingdom burials contained wooden funerary models depicting figures producing food as a way of provisioning the dead. Images of food production, such as baking or brewing, which had been previously depicted on tomb walls, were now also made in model form. While this was a new form of representation, the underlying idea of nourishing the dead remained the same.

Reverence for ancestors is woven into the fabric of Chinese life. The relationship between the living and those who went before them is sustained partly through offerings, including food. In China, there is a long-held belief

These model food dishes contain the ingredients for a feast of the soul in the afterlife and give us an idea of the foods that were eaten by the living in the Ming era. Each of the major food groups – meat, poultry, fish, vegetables and cereals – is present.

Model offering dishes, c. 1400–1600. Shaanxi, China. Earthenware. H. 4.5 cm, Diam. 11.7 cm. 1927,1214.7. Donated by Lady Edith Chester Beatty.

Left, top: The Day of the Dead, when families welcome back the souls of their ancestors, is widely celebrated in Mexico. This model altar (*ofrenda*) is a miniature version of the tables spread with food and drink with which families greet the souls, weary and hungry after their long journey.

Miniature altar, 1970s. Puebla, Mexico. Wood, pottery. H. 9 cm, W. 12 cm, D. 7.5 cm. Am1978,15.630.

Left, bottom: In ancient Egypt, the provision of offerings was central to the survival of the deceased in the next world. On this wooden funerary stela, Deniuenkhonsu – for whom the stela was made – worships a falcon-headed god named Ra-Horakhty-Atum. Her offerings include lotuses, a plucked, eviscerated fowl, grapes, bread, cos lettuces and a jar of beer.

Stela, 22nd Dynasty, *c.* 800 BCE. Thebes, Egypt. Painted sycamore-fig wood. H. 33 cm, W. 27 cm, D. 4 cm. EA 27332.

that edible offerings represent a way of interacting with the spirit world. In honouring one's ancestors, ensuring that they are not forgotten and that they receive the provisions they need to sustain them, the hope is they will intercede in one's favour in the spirit world. Food offerings to the ancestors are presented on altars, and the favourite foods of deceased relatives are placed on their grave. Food and models of food were placed in graves to feed the souls in the afterlife. An inventory of the Han-dynasty Mawangdui tombs in Hunan province lists provisions including twenty-four cauldrons filled with *geng* (a thick soup; see also page 199) made from game and fish. Chinese funerary goods on sale today include models of such dishes as roast duck and dim sum.

In Mexico, the Day of the Dead holiday in November is widely celebrated. During the festivities, families visit the graves of their ancestors, bringing with them offerings of their favourite foods for their spirits to enjoy. Homemade altars known as *ofrendas* are set up in houses, and the favourite food and drink of the dead relatives is placed on them alongside photographs of the deceased and Mexican marigolds.

Left: In Judaism, kosher foods are those allowed and prepared by laws and traditions set out in the Torah, the first five books of the Hebrew Bible. Labels certify the proper preparation of food and make it easy to keep kosher and non-kosher foods separate from one another while in storage.

Food label, 17th–18th century. Russia. Lead. L. 4.5 cm. 1987,0607.5.

Below left: This eighteenth-century illustration depicts two important Jewish customs: the preparation for Passover, which commemorates the Exodus; and the Passover feast, or Seder. The latter is marked by the serving of special, symbolic foods, among them a lamb shank bone, bitter herbs, a roasted egg, matzo bread and charoset (a fruit-and-nut paste).

Bernard Picart, illustration to *Cérémonies et coutumes religieuses de tous les peuples du monde* (Religious ceremonies and customs of all peoples of the world), 1725. France. Etching and engraving on paper. H. 33.5 cm, W. 22.4 cm. 1917,1208.1493. Donated by Nan Ino Cooper, Baroness Lucas of Crudwell and Lady Dingwall, in Memory of Auberon Thomas Herbert, 9th Baron Lucas of Crudwell and 5th Lord Dingwall.

RELIGION · CUSTOMS AND TRADITIONS

Right: This bowl, of a kind known as *zlafah*, is used particularly for serving harira soup, a Moroccan speciality made from meat, lentils, chickpeas, rice and fragrant spices. Traditionally, the soup is served after the breaking of the daily fast undertaken by Muslims each year during the period of Ramadan.

Soup bowl, *c.* 1992. Workshop of Moulay Ahmed Serghini, Morocco. Ceramic. H. 8.5 cm, Diam. 19 cm. Af1992,01.9.

Below: In Māori culture, feeding funnels such as this one are known as *korere*. They were used to pass liquids and pureed foods into the mouths of people who were observing strict sacred restrictions and protocols. It is also believed they were used when someone was receiving a facial tattoo.

Feeding funnel, *c.* 1820. Hokianga, New Zealand. Wood, haliotis shell. H. 14.5 cm, W. 16.5 cm, D. 10.5 cm. Oc1915,0217.4.

The three individuals in this hanging scroll are Confucius, Buddha and Laozi, founders of Confucianism, Buddhism and Taoism respectively. They are shown tasting vinegar, and their expressions – in turn sour, bitter and sweet – are intended to reflect their philosophies, with Buddhism seeing life as bitter, dominated by pain and suffering.

Kano Eitoku Tachinobu, after Kano Masanobu, three vinegar tasters, 1800–80. Japan. Painted silk scroll. H. 127 cm, W. 50 cm. 1881,1210,0.1548.

Right, top: The alms bowl – an example of which can be seen at the base of this ivory figure – is an important object for Buddhist monks. The alms placed in such bowls by lay people include food for sustenance. For the donors, the giving of alms supports the monks in their study and practice of Buddhism and is an act of charity with a spiritual dimension.

Figure, 19th–20th century. China. Ivory, wood. H. 18 cm. 2018,3005.173. Donated by the Sir Victor Sassoon Chinese Ivories Trust.

Right, bottom: This type of water sprinkler was used for ritual cleansing. The lotus scroll around the body of the sprinkler is a common ornament on fifteenth- and sixteenth-century Chinese cloisonné vessels. It is especially appropriate for those connected with Buddhist ritual as it symbolizes purity.

Kundika water sprinkler, 1426–35. China. Bronze, enamel, gold. H. 20.3 cm. 1977,0718.1. Donated by Sir Harry M. Garner and Lady Garner, in honour of Douglas Barrett.

Eggs symbolize new life and the arrival of spring. For Christians, they also represent the shape of the tomb in which Jesus was buried. For more than five hundred years, Christians in eastern Europe, Russia and Siberia have decorated chicken eggs at Easter. This example from Poland has a pattern applied in wax.

Easter eggs, 1974–79. Poland. Eggshell, wax. H. 5.4–5.9 cm. 2018.8050.135-140. Donated by John Newall.

Left: The Stonyhurst Salt, an elaborate salt holder composed of enamelled silver gilt, rock crystal, rubies and garnets, hides a secret. The materials from which it is made come from older religious objects used in the Catholic Church. When these objects were banned by the Protestant Reformation, their component parts were reused for secular objects, rather than being destroyed.

Salt holder, made by John Robinson (?), 1577–78. London, UK. Rock crystal, ruby, garnet, enamel, silver. H. 26.3 cm, Diam. 9.4 cm. 1958,1004.1. Purchase funded with contribution from Art Fund (as NACF).

Above: Here, St Elizabeth of Hungary gives bread to someone in need, in accordance with Christian values. In a popular legend about the saint, when she was questioned by her husband, the loaves she was hiding beneath her cloak turned miraculously into roses.

Print, St Elizabeth of Hungary, 1465–75. Germany. Woodcut with hand-colouring on paper. H. 7.3 cm, W. 5.4 cm. 1930,1217.4.

RELIGION • CHRISTIANITY

Feasts

Feasting, the coming-together of people to share a special meal, is a practice found in societies around the world. Feasts are held for a variety of reasons: religious or political; to celebrate an event, perhaps a coronation or military victory; for transactional or economic motives; to entertain, impress or bring together a community. Often, feasts have a noticeably structured aspect, governed by rules and rituals.

The very idea of a feast contains within it notions of excess and luxury. The food at feasts must be served in generous, even excessive, quantities; in many cultures, the leftovers are shared with the poor. The food must also be distinctive, as different as possible from everyday fare. Traditionally, no expense is spared on the ingredients, while rare and exotic foodstuffs are prized for the distinction they bring to the meal.

Not only should the ingredients at banquets be out of the ordinary, so too should the skill with which they are prepared. In China, for example, dazzling displays of knife work, including ornamental carvings, have long been part of the banqueting tradition. A Chinese banquet features a range of dishes, designed to showcase the talents of the chefs. The tableware at banquets is also designed to impress, made by talented craftspeople from precious materials, such as metals, gemstones and fine porcelain. In medieval and Renaissance Europe, diners at banquets were entertained between courses by ingenious, visually striking *soltelties* (subtleties) – ornamental set pieces, some edible and others purely decorative – and theatrical displays. A banquet held in 1527 by England's Cardinal Wolsey for the French ambassador at court featured more than a hundred subtleties, including representations of St Paul's Cathedral, animals and a chessboard.

Throughout history, one can find accounts of spectacular royal banquets marked by phenomenal quantities of food. In 879 BCE, at Nimrud in modern-day Iraq, the Assyrian king Ashurnasirpal II held a grand banquet to inaugurate his new capital. According to records, the banquet lasted ten days, during which time the 69,574 guests consumed 2,000 oxen and calves, 16,000 sheep and goats, 10,000 pigeons and 10,000 skins of wine. Many centuries later, at their meeting at the Field of the Cloth of Gold in 1520, Henry VIII of England and Francis I of France attempted to outshine each other with impressive banquets and lavish entertainment. The excessive consumption of fine foods by royalty, the aristocratic and the wealthy was a way of emphasizing and maintaining the social hierarchy.

Marriages are another example of the events that are commonly celebrated with a feast. In India, among both Hindu and Muslim communities, the wedding banquet is an important occasion, with the quality and quantity of the food on offer a source of social prestige. While among orthodox Hindus and Brahmins the wedding food is vegetarian, a Muslim wedding banquet features meat dishes, including at least one biriyani. In Britain, the centrepiece of a wedding feast is the wedding cake – traditionally cut by the bride and groom and shared among the guests celebrating their marriage.

Elaborate feasts played an important part in the lives of the Etruscan aristocracy and – as funerary banquets – in their deaths. Stone-relief sculptures depicting banqueting scenes appear on the sides of Etruscan sarcophagi and funerary urns. This bronze statuette of a reclining male banqueter holding a libation bowl belongs in a funerary context.

Figure, 500–480 BCE. Italy. Bronze.
H. 15.6 cm, W. 9.5 cm, L. 32.8 cm.
1831,1201.1.

Above: In the Roman world, the celebratory consumption of food and drink was an important social ritual. As in the Greek world, guests at Roman banquets reclined on couches, where they were served with food and drink by servants. Here, a reclining man wearing a wreath – a symbol of triumph – drinks from a horn.

Wall-paint fragment, 50–79 CE. Italy. Possibly plaster. H. 14.5 cm, W. 21.5 cm. 1856,1226.1623. Bequeathed by Sir William Temple.

Below: In this regal garden scene, the Neo-Assyrian king Ashurbanipal reclines on a sofa beneath a vine, his enthroned queen sitting opposite, while servants fan them both. The couple are toasting wine with refreshments on the table. Hanging from a tree behind the queen is the severed head of Teumman, king of Elam, Ashurbanipal's vanquished enemy.

Relief wall panel, 645–635 BCE. Nineveh, Iraq. Gypsum. H. 58.4 cm, W. 139.7 cm, D. 15.2 cm. 1856,0909.53.

Dating from the early Islamic period, this gilded silver plate depicts a princely figure having a picnic. He reclines on a cushioned mattress, with servants and musicians in attendance. Around him are items for the feast: wine jars in a cooler, an animal-hide water bottle, a pot cooking over a fire and a grape vine overhead.

Dish, 7th–8th century. Tabaristan, northeast Iran. Gold, silver. H. 4 cm, Diam. 20 cm. 1963,1210.3. Bequeathed by Sir Augustus Wollaston Franks.

From 1189, coronation banquets for newly crowned British monarchs were held in Westminster Hall. As this print clearly shows, George IV's 1821 coronation banquet was a lavish affair. It was the last one held in the hall, as the custom was deemed too expensive.

Robert Havell II, *The Royal Banquet*, 1824. Published in London, UK. Aquatint with hand-colouring on paper. H. 40 cm, W. 50 cm. 1867,1012.812.

In Japan during the Heian period (794–1185), the practice developed among the aristocracy of holding nocturnal banquets while contemplating the beauty of the autumn full moon. Moon-viewing parties still take place in Japan, with certain foods, including mooncakes, eaten in celebration.

Kitagawa Utamaro, banquet for gazing at the autumn moon, *c.* 1775–80. Japan. Colour woodblock print on paper. H. 21.5 cm, W. 32 cm. 1906,1220,0.317.

FASTING

The antithesis of indulging in a feast is the act of choosing to go without food. In many of the world's major religions, the two practices have long been connected. When one looks at religions like Hinduism, Christianity, Judaism and Islam, one finds that their calendars are marked by a pattern of both ritual fasting and ritual feasting. Indeed, the end of a period of fasting – during which one eats either very little or no food at all – is customarily followed by a celebratory feast.

In the Christian calendar, the forty days between Ash Wednesday and Easter form a period of fasting known as Lent, instituted in remembrance of Christ's forty-day fast in the desert. Traditionally, on the day before this period of abstention, Shrove Tuesday or Mardi Gras (Fat Tuesday), people enjoy some of the food and drink that will soon be prohibited. In Britain, for example, Shrove Tuesday is marked by the making of pancakes, as a way of using up eggs, milk and butter. In other countries, including Brazil, Trinidad and Tobago, and Italy, the days before Ash Wednesday are filled with celebratory festivals known as carnivals. It is thought that the root of the word 'carnival' might be the Latin phrase *carnem levare*, meaning to remove meat. The end of Lent, a period of renunciation, is marked with a special Easter meal traditionally featuring such symbolic foods as lamb and eggs.

Giovedi Grasso, or 'Fat Thursday', is an important day in Venice's carnival calendar. Historically, the celebration in St Mark's Square on this day marked a victory by the Serenissima Republic of Venice over the Patriarch of Aquileia and featured the symbolic slaughtering of animals sent in tribute.

Print, 1610. Published in Venice, Italy. Engraving on paper. H. 24.7 cm, W. 15.6 cm. 1868,0822.8557. Bequeathed by Felix Slade.

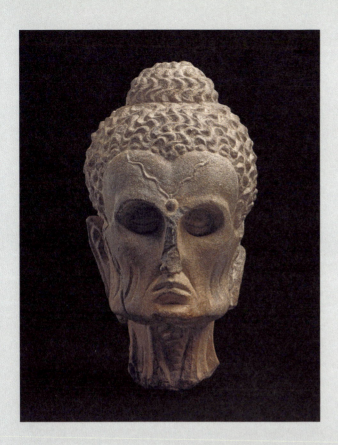

There is a stark power to this gaunt head of the fasting Buddha. In order to gain enlightenment, the Buddha practised a regime of strict austerity and fasting. When this failed, he rejected such austere measures in favour of the Middle Way, a practice that avoids the extremes of both asceticism and indulgence.

Figure, 2nd–3rd century CE. Pakistan. Schist. H. 22.3 cm, W. 12.7 cm, Diam. 18.5 cm. 1907,1228.1. Donated by Col. F. G. Mainwaring.

Fasting is an important part of the Hindu faith. In the sacred literature of Hinduism, the *Bhavishya Purana* prescribes more than 130 fasts a year. Fasting is carried out for a variety of reasons: as a petition to a god or an act of self-discipline or cleansing, or as part of a religious festival. Women, who are charged with looking after the ritual purity of the family's food and kitchen, fast more than men. Mourning in many cultures is often a period marked by fasting. In Hinduism, when a parent or close relative dies, all eating and cooking activities in the bereaved household cease until the body is cremated. A period of fasting follows, which ends with a feast held for family and friends. The Indian independence leader Mahatma Gandhi added a political dimension to the traditional act of fasting. As part of his philosophy of non-violent resistance, *satyagraha*, he undertook fasts – including one lasting twenty-one days – for different reasons, including as a form of penance, in opposition to the British, and in protest against communal violence.

In Islam, one of the five basic tenets, or 'pillars', is the injunction to fast during Ramadan, the ninth month of the Muslim calendar. During this time, Muslims refrain from eating, drinking, smoking and sex from sunrise to sunset. The daily fast is broken with a small snack called *iftar*, often including dates, which were eaten by the Prophet Muhammad to break his fast. Eid al-Fitr, the end of Ramadan, is celebrated with communal feasts. Certain dishes are traditionally enjoyed at Eid, among them *saviya*, a dessert made from vermicelli fried in ghee, milk and sugar.

Above: Wooden sculptures of wild geese, known as *gireogi*, played an important part in traditional Korean wedding ceremonies. They trace their origins to the practice of a bridegroom offering a live goose to the bride's mother, as a symbol of fidelity. Wooden geese, wrapped in *bojagi* (wrapping cloth), later replaced the use of live birds.

Figure, 19th century. Korea. Wood. H. 18 cm, W. 29 cm. 1991,1220.1.

Below: Across many cultures, the main celebratory event of a marriage has been a special meal enjoyed by the families and friends of the couple. This Limoges enamelled dish, made in France in the mid- to late sixteenth century, shows the gods on Mount Olympus celebrating a wedding with a feast.

Dish, attributed to Jean de Court, *c*. 1555–85. Limoges, France. Copper, enamel, gold. H. 38.5 cm, W. 52.4 cm, D. 5.8 cm. 1885,0508.16. Donated by Sir Andrew Fountaine.

The marriage feast at Cana, a story in the Gospel of John, features the first miracle attributed to Jesus Christ. In the story, Jesus and his mother, Mary, attend a wedding feast. When the wine runs out, Jesus turns water into wine.

Master of the Martyrdom of the Ten Thousand, the marriage at Cana, 1460–70. Germany. Engraving with hand-colouring on paper. H. 13.5 cm, W. 9.5 cm. 1846,0709.29.

Left: The Persian inscription on this plate expresses the desire for good fortune: 'May this dish always be full of blessings from halal riches / May it always be in the company of fortunate people / May this dish never be empty of blessings'.

Dish, 1677–78. Kirman, Iran. Stonepaste. H. 9 cm, Diam. 40.5 cm. G.308. Bequeathed by Miss Edith Godman.

Below: Large bowls such as this one were used at funerals in the Solomon Islands. They held a savoury, pudding-like dish. Made from taro roots, cassava or sweet potato, and often mixed with coconut milk to make a paste, the dish would have been baked in an earth oven.

Bowl, 19th century. Makira, Solomon Islands. Wood, cone shell, nut-putty. H. 62 cm, W. 58.5 cm, L. 187.5 cm. Oc1990,Q.86.

Whether made to serve delicacies or just for show, the Roman British Mildenhall Great Dish depicts a terrific party fuelled by wine provided by the god Bacchus. Even Hercules, renowned for his great strength, staggers under the influence of alcohol and has to be supported by satyrs.

Mildenhall Great Dish, 4th century CE. Mildenhall, UK. Silver. H. 6.1 cm, Diam. 60.5 cm. 1946,1007.1.

Above: Dating to the late thirteenth century, this bronze aquamanile – from the Latin for water (*aqua*) and hand (*manus*) – takes the form of a knight on his horse. Likely made for pouring the water used in the washing of hands at mealtimes, aquamaniles would have been striking features of the medieval dining table.

Aquamanile, c. 1275–1300. Hexham, UK. Copper alloy. H. 33.3 cm, W. 25 cm, D. 11.2 cm. 1853,0315.1.

Right: Featuring the form of a horned, winged griffin, this gilt silver rhyton (a type of drinking vessel shaped in part like an animal) is one of the most famous examples of silverware from the Achaemenid empire. It was originally used to pour wine, with the lowermost hole in the griffin's chest acting as the pourer. Rhyta were symbols of high status, used at royal banquets.

Rhyton, 5th century BCE. Altintepe, eastern Turkey. Silver, gold. H. 23 cm, Diam. 14.5 cm. 1897,1231.178. Bequeathed by Sir Augustus Wollaston Franks.

Right, top: Taking the form of a ship, a nef was an elaborate table ornament intended to delight the guests at medieval and Renaissance banquets. This example, made in Augsburg, Germany, in the late sixteenth century, incorporates automata and a small chiming clock. The former enabled it to move along the table, play a tune and fire a series of tiny canons.

Nef, made by Hans Schlottheim, 1580–90. Augsburg, Germany. Brass, iron, silver, enamel. H. 104 cm, W. 20.3 cm, D. 78.5 cm. 1866,1030.1. Donated by Octavius Morgan.

Right, bottom: Impressing your guests with lavish tableware has a long tradition. This pair of flagons, dating from the first millennium BCE, was found in Basse-Yutz, France. The flagons have an Etruscan shape elaborated with Celtic patterns and animal images, and were probably used for pouring wine. The copper-alloy bodies are decorated at the spout and foot with inlaid coral and red glass.

Flagons, c. 420–360 BCE. Basse-Yutz, France. Copper alloy, coral, glass. H. 39.6–40.6 cm. 1929,0511.1-2. Purchase funded with contribution from Art Fund (as NACF); Lord Melchett (Alfred Mond); F. A. Szarvasy; Sir Percival David, 2nd Baronet; Sir Alfred Chester Beatty; Calouste Sarkis Gulbenkian; John Duncan Vaughan Campbell, 5th Earl Cawdor; Lycett Green; John Hugh Smith; and Prof Tancred Borenius.

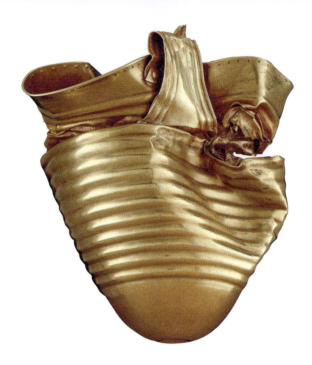

Left, top: This small, handled cup – known as the Ringlemere Cup after the farm in southeast England where it was found – is one of a small number of its kind, made from gold, amber or shale almost 4,000 years ago. Rare and special, such objects probably replaced pottery cups at important events, perhaps for the serving of mead.

Cup, 1950–1750 BCE. Ringlemere Farm, Kent, UK. Gold. H. 11.2 cm, W. 10.5 cm. 2003,0501.1. Acquired through the Treasure Act with contribution from Art Fund (as NACF), Heritage Lottery Fund and British Museum Friends.

Left, bottom: The remarkable Lycurgus Cup was made in the fourth century CE by a Roman glass-maker, presumably for a great person or occasion. The glass contains nano particles of gold and silver, which cause the glass to change colour from red to green depending on whether light is transmitted through it or reflected off it.

Cup, 4th century CE. Findspot unknown. Glass, silver. H. 15.8 cm, Diam. 13.2 cm. 1958,1202.1. Purchased funded with contribution from Art Fund (as NACF).

Right: This is one of fourteen complete glass beakers known as the Hedwig glasses. Made in the twelfth century, the beakers take their name from St Hedwig of Silesia (d. 1243), with whom three of them are associated. According to legend, when Hedwig, Duchess of Silesia, drank water from a beaker, it turned into wine.

Beaker, 12th century. Possibly made in Syria. Glass. H. 12.5 cm, Diam. 12 cm. 1959,0414.1. Purchase funded by P. T. Brooke Sewell, Esq.

Left: Impressive tableware from the medieval period is rare: as fashions changed, the silver and gold from which they were made were melted down and used to make different objects. Exquisite in the simplicity of its form, the fifteenth-century Lacock Cup is beautifully decorated with ropework around its foot, stem and lid.

Cup, 15th century. UK. Silver, gold. H. 35 cm, Diam. 13.8 cm. 2014,8002.1. Purchased in memory of Melvin R. Seiden, with contribution from National Heritage Memorial Fund, John Studzinski, Art Fund, American Friends of the British Museum, British Museum Friends, Jean Sibley (bequest), Headley Trust, and Roberta Ahmanson and Howard Ahmanson jointly.

Alcohol

People have consumed and enjoyed alcoholic drinks for thousands of years. Alcohol is a drug that affects the brain, causing inebriation. Depending on the level of consumption, drinking alcohol can lower inhibitions, resulting in people feeling relaxed and cheerful, but it also has depressive and narcotic properties. The intoxicating qualities of alcoholic drinks – allowing the mind to reach a different state – have given them a special status, and in some cultures they were used in rituals and as libations to the gods. Alcoholic drinks are so highly regarded that, to this day, special tableware is used not only for their consumption, but also to cool and serve them.

Alcohol is made by fermenting such foodstuffs as honey, fruits, vegetables and grains. During the fermentation process, microscopic yeasts break down the sugar molecules in these foods, producing both ethanol (alcohol) and carbon dioxide. The human partiality for alcohol is such that, around the world, one finds alcoholic beverages made from a variety of local ingredients: rum from sugar cane, *chicha* from maize, palm wine from the sap of palm trees, beer from barley, cider from apples, and wine from grapes. Spirits are made by taking alcoholic drinks produced through fermentation and distilling them. The process of distillation concentrates the alcohol, resulting in drinks with a high alcoholic content. Distillation is an ancient practice, associated with alchemy; distilled drinks, including aqua vitae, were made in monasteries and considered to have medicinal properties. The pot still, a piece of equipment developed for distilling centuries ago, remains in use by the drinks industry today.

The deleterious effects of alcohol on human behaviour and health, as well as its addictive nature, have long been a concern. A number of religions, among them Islam and Jainism, prohibit its consumption, while observant Buddhists avoid consuming alcohol as doing so would violate one of the Five Precepts. Other religions, while permitting it, call for its consumption to be moderate. Temperance movements, promoting abstinence from alcohol, have been a powerful social force in a number of countries. In the twentieth century, the United States passed laws preventing the manufacture, sale and transportation of alcoholic beverages within its borders, a period known as the Prohibition era (1920–early 1930s). The restrictions, however, backfired, resulting in the rise of the illegal production and drinking of alcohol, which benefitted organized crime.

Despite its known side-effects, alcohol remains central to socializing in many societies. Taverns, inns, beer halls, pubs and bars provide dedicated public spaces where people can enjoy alcoholic drinks together. The desire for alcohol is catered for by a profitable global drinks industry, with the market projected to grow. Some alcoholic beverages, including champagne and cocktails, are seen as celebratory, and alcohol is often used to mark such special occasions as weddings, christenings and birthday parties.

Left: This Peruvian ceremonial vessel, or *paccha*, has been made in the form of a foot plough. The vessel is hollow and has an opening at the top, into which *chicha* (fermented maize beer) would have been poured; the liquid would have then emerged from a small hole at the tip of the vessel, symbolically irrigating and fertilizing the earth.

Vessel, 1400–1532. Peru. Pottery. H. 42.3 cm, W. 22.6 cm, D. 13.6 cm. Am1947,10.39. Donated by Mrs E. H. Spottiswoode.

Below: Stoneware jugs or bottles were common items of functional tableware in the late sixteenth to early seventeenth century. Made from pottery fired at high temperatures to produce a hard, impermeable surface, often with the image of a bearded man, they were used for trading, storing and the serving of wine, beer, cider, oil, vinegar, water or even homemade 'witch potions'.

Jug, c. 1590–1600. Made in Frechen, Germany, found in London, UK. Stoneware. H. 23.7 cm, Diam. 9.6 cm. 1856,0701.1615.
Jug, c. 1590–1600. Made in Frechen, Germany, found in London, UK. Stoneware. H. 17.2 cm, Diam. 8 cm (base). 1854,0422.1.
Jug, 1599. Made in Frechen, Germany, found in the North Sea. Stoneware. H. 22 cm, Diam. 9.5 cm (base). 1910,1215.1. Donated by Col. Alfred J. Copeland.

Left: Netsuke – small, decorative toggles – often featured aspects of Japanese culture, such as religious subjects, animals and the country's myths and folklore. In this piece, two inebriated *shojo*, sea sprites with a fondness for alcohol, are clambering around a *sake* bottle.

Netsuke, early 19th century. Japan. Ivory. H. 4.5 cm, W. 3.6 cm, D. 2.3 cm. S.48.

Right: Beer in ancient Egypt was seen as essential, provided as a ration to labourers like those who built the pyramids in Giza. Ceramic vessels, like this pottery beer jar, were key to the ancient Egyptian fermenting process, as their porous interiors offered a suitable surface on which the wild yeast culture could grow.

Beer jar, Second Intermediate Period, *c.* 1750–1550 BCE. Esna, Egypt. Pottery. H. 23.1 cm, Diam. 15 cm. EA 42108. Donated by Frederick George Hilton Price.

BEER

The alcoholic beverage called beer has been made and drunk for thousands of years. It remains popular to this day, and is the world's most widely consumed alcoholic drink. Historically, beer – which is a fermented drink – was seen as offering a safer alternative to polluted water. Grains, notably barley, are the starting point for beer, which is produced through the action of yeast fermenting the grains. In order to trigger this fermentation process, it is necessary first to treat the grains and break down their starch to sugars. A process called malting was developed, in which grain is soaked in water, germinated, and then heated with ungerminated grain. Barley is the preferred grain for beer-making because of its capacity to generate starch-consuming enzymes. The Incas used a different technique for triggering the fermentation process in grain. Ground maize was chewed, with the enzymes found in human saliva turning the starch into sugar; this chewed maize was then mixed with cooked maize and fermented into a form of beer called *chicha*. The ancient Egyptians, Sumerians and Babylonians made beer using baked loaves of barley bread soaked in water to form the 'mash' – the start of the brewing process.

In northern Europe, where grapes could not be grown but barley could, beer became an important drink. The Roman historians Tacitus and Pliny recorded the Germanic tribes making a fermented drink from barley or wheat. During the early Middle Ages, monasteries were major producers of beer in Europe.

Beer has been drunk and enjoyed in Germany for many years. Traditionally it was served in a stein, a stoneware beer mug with a hinged lid – here made from pewter – to keep insects out. The rustic practicality of the stein's shape has endured over the centuries, and it is made in Germany to this day.

Beer tankard, designed by Paul Wynand, made by R. Merkelbach, c. 1909–14. Grenzhausen, Germany. Stoneware. H. 14.3 cm, W. 14.9 cm. 1993,1105.2. Donated by Graham Dry.

The making of beer has developed over the centuries, laying the foundation for the methods used today. Traditionally, beer was flavoured with various herbs. In around 900 CE, in Bavaria, aromatic hop cones (also called hop flowers) were added to the drink. It was discovered that not only did the hops add a pleasant fragrance, they also, crucially, extended beer's shelf life considerably, allowing it to be transported. Another important Bavarian discovery, this time in around 1400 CE, was an alternative way of fermenting beer. Rather than fermenting it quickly over a few days, as had been the norm, a much slower method was adopted in which the beer was fermented in cool caves, developing a yeast that grew below the surface of the liquid. This mild-flavoured beer was known as lager, from the German *lager*, meaning 'storeroom'. The eighteenth century saw further innovations, including the creation in England of a dark, strong beer known as porter. Recent decades have seen the rise of a craft-beer brewing scene in countries around the world, with micro-breweries producing their own, distinctive beers.

In ancient Egypt, particularly during the Middle Kingdom (*c.* 2055–1650 BCE), wooden models of food production were placed in tombs to provide a means of sustaining the dead in the afterlife. This model of a baking and brewing scene would have ensured that the deceased had a perpetual supply of beer.

Model group, 11th Dynasty, *c.* 2050–2000 BCE. Deir el-Bahri, Thebes, Egypt. Wood. H. 25.5 cm, W. 79.5 cm, D. 48 cm. EA 40915. Donated by Egypt Exploration Fund.

The Mughal emperor Jahangir was an avid collector of Timurid objects, including carved jade pieces. When he acquired this vessel, he commissioned an inscription to be carved on it consisting of his name, the date, and verses referring to the drinking of wine.

Cup, 1618–19. India. Nephrite. H. 10.3 cm. Diam. 13 cm. 1945,1017.257. Bequeathed by Oscar Charles Raphael.

Above: The different flower motifs on these porcelain wine cups – decorated in underglaze blue and translucent overglaze colours – relate to the twelve months of the lunar year. Each cup also bears a couplet ending with the character *shang* (meaning 'appreciation' or 'reward').

Set of twelve wine cups, 1662–1722. Jingdezhen, China. Glazed porcelain. H. 5 cm, Diam. 6.5 cm. PDF.815. On loan to the British Museum from the Sir Percival David Collection.

Right: This elegant stag resting its forefeet on a shield is a virtuoso piece made from silver gilt. The body is hollow, designed to contain wine or brandy, which may then be sipped from a cup formed by taking off the stag's head and turning it over.

Standing cup, 1500–1600. Vienna, Austria. Silver. H. 27.5 cm, W. 9.4 cm, D. 19.3 cm. WB.138. Bequeathed by Baron Ferdinand Anselm Rothschild.

WINE

People have been turning naturally sweet liquids into alcoholic drinks by fermenting them – apple juice into cider, honey water into mead – for centuries. The juice of grapes (known as must) is the starting point for wine, an alcoholic drink with a venerable history. Wild yeasts grow naturally on the skin of grapes. When these yeasts come into contact with grape juice, a fermentation process begins that produces an alcoholic liquid rich in compounds, creating aroma and flavours. Among the early evidence of wine-making are the grape seeds, tannins and tartaric wine residues found in pieces of a *qvevri* (a Georgian earthenware vessel used for winemaking) in Georgia dating back 8,000 years.

Many ancient societies contributed to the knowledge of both viticulture (grape-growing) and viniculture (wine-making). In ancient Egypt, wines were stored in sealed amphoras that allowed the wine to age for years without oxidizing; wine amphoras found in the tombs of the pharaohs have labels giving details of when and where the wine was made. Wine was an important drink in ancient Greece. The Greeks did much to popularize vine-growing and wine-making around the cities they established across the Mediterranean, even naming a region of southern Italy Oenotria (the land

In ancient Greece, a symposium was a social gathering at which members of the male social elite reclined on couches while drinking wine, conversing with one another and being entertained by musicians and dancers. In this depiction of a symposium, one man holds a *kylix*, a cup with a stem, while a second raises a *phiale*, a shallow drinking bowl.

Krater, c. 450–440 BCE. Made in Athens, Greece, said to have been excavated at Nola, Italy. Pottery. H. 34.3 cm, Diam. 27.9 cm. 1867,0508.1135.

Venice has long been famous for its skilfully made, colourful glass-ware. In 1291, for reasons of security and to reduce the risk of fire, the Republic of Venice moved its glass production to the island of Murano. Among the items produced on Murano were wine glasses, such as this seventeenth-century engraved example, which would have sparkled on the wealthiest tables.

Wine glass, late 17th century. Venice, Italy. Glass. H. 17.7 cm. S.439. Bequeathed by Felix Slade.

of vines). The Romans are credited with adding considerably to the knowledge of viticulture, improving methods of vine cultivation. Both vine-growing and wine-making expanded with the Roman Empire, with new vineyards established to meet the demand for wine from garrisons and Roman citizens. The Romans focused on identifying the land in Gaul and the Rhineland best suited for vineyards; most of today's important wine regions in France and Germany bear traces of Roman influence. Following the fall of the Roman Empire, monasteries in Europe preserved and progressed the understanding of viticulture and viniculture; in Christianity, wine is required for the sacrament of Communion. A significant development in wine's history during the seventeenth century was the use of corks to seal the wine bottles, helping to prevent the harmful effects of oxygen on the quality of wine while allowing wines to be matured successfully.

Wine is rich in cultural significance, used ritually in such religions as Judaism and Christianity. The ancient Greeks developed the cult of the god Dionysus (known as Bacchus by the Romans), whose followers took part in ecstatic revelries fuelled by the drinking of wine. Today, wine is still considered a special drink, with wine connoisseurs held in high regard. It is enjoyed both as a drink in its own right and as one to be consumed with food. Sparkling wines, notably champagne, are often drunk on celebratory occasions, including weddings, birthdays and anniversaries.

Above: Part of the Anglo-Saxon ship burial unearthed at Sutton Hoo, these bands of silver gilt, decorated with birds and animals, fitted onto the tips and rims of long, twisted horns used in drinking rituals. The horns, from wild cattle called aurochs, were a powerful symbol of masculinity and held about a litre of ale or mead.

Drinking-horn fittings, mounted onto a replica horn, early 7th century. Sutton Hoo, UK. Silver, plaster (for reconstruction). Diam. 9.5 cm. 1939,1010.120, 1939,1010.121. Donated by Mrs Edith M. Pretty.

Below: Metal straws have become fashionable in the fight against disposable plastic straws. This metal drinking straw, decorated with gold and lapis lazuli, was made in the historic city of Ur in 2600 BCE. Long tubes were used for drinking liquids, such as beer, that might have had scum floating on the surface.

Drinking straw, 2600 BCE. Ur, Iraq. Gold, lapis lazuli, silver, bitumen, copper. Diam. 0.9 cm, L. 87.6 cm. 1928,1010.95.

Above: Scenes of eating and drinking are depicted on this marble cylinder seal. In the top part, a woman receives a cup from an attendant while two others stand behind her, and a man drinks through a straw from a large vessel that likely contained beer.

Cylinder seal, 2600 BCE. Ur, Iraq. Marble. H. 3.6 cm, Diam. 1.7 cm. 1930,1213.130.

Right: This Chinese-style blue-and-white bowl with lid was made in Europe at the end of the seventeenth century and used for serving punch, traditionally a mixture of wine or spirits, fruit juices, sugar and spices. Its decoration shows themes of drinking alcohol with Bacchus, the god of wine, and tavern scenes.

Punch bowl, 1697. Probably made in London, UK. Earthenware. H. 36.3 cm, Diam. 31.4 cm. 1911,0712.2. Donated by Max Rosenheim, through Art Fund (as NACF).

Right: As statement pieces on the dinner table of a wealthy aristocrat, these gold ice buckets, with their regal lion heads holding hinged loop handles, must have looked magnificent. Known as the Marlborough Ice Pails, they once formed part of the many treasures given to the first Duke and Duchess of Marlborough.

Pair of ice buckets, *c.* 1700. UK. Gold. H. 26.7–26.9 cm, Diam. 21.7–21.8 cm. 1981,1201.1-2. Purchase funded with contribution from National Heritage Memorial Fund, Art Fund (as NACF), Worshipful Company of Goldsmiths, Pilgrim Trust and funds bequeathed by Mrs Katherine Goodhart-Kitchingman.

Above: This sphinx-handled maiolica-ware bowl decorated with charming putti and, inside, a scene depicting Moses striking water from the rock at Horeb was an artful container for keeping a bottle of wine chilled using cold water rather than ice. The evaporation of the water created a cooling effect.

Bowl, probably by the Patanazzi Family, *c.* 1580–1610. Urbino, Italy. Earthenware. H. 26 cm, W. 64.5 cm, Diam. 49.5 cm. WB.60. Bequeathed by Baron Ferdinand Anselm Rothschild.

This double-walled *psykter* (wine-cooler) is in the shape of a belly-amphora, decorated with a mythological scene depicting Dionysus surrounded by his entourage of satyrs and maenads. The spout in the outer wall allowed cold water or pieces of ice to be poured into the hollow space between the walls, cooling the wine inside.

Psykter wine-cooler, *c.* 560–540 BCE. Made in Athens, Greece, probably excavated in Italy. Pottery. H. 32 cm, W. 23 cm. 1848,0619.5.

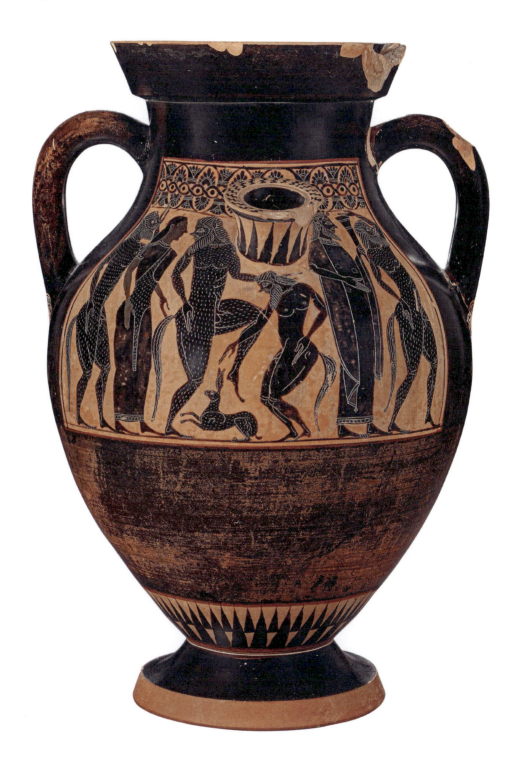

RICE WINE

The term 'rice wine' is used generically to describe a distinctive form of grain-based alcohol first developed thousands of years ago in China. While wine made from grapes is produced by fermenting grape juice, the making of rice wine involves a number of stages. The first step is to break the grain down into fermentable sugars. This is done through the introduction to the cooked rice of a special microbial mixture called *qu*, which supplies starch-digesting enzymes. The *qu* used to make Chinese wines is made from ground grains and pulses, which are moistened and kept in dark, humid conditions to encourage the growth of various moulds, including *Aspergillus* and *Mucor*, and yeasts. Once the *qu* has reached the desired level of mould growth, it is dried and used as needed. There are detailed, written instructions for cultivating *qu* dating back to the sixth century in China, giving examples of the *qu* varieties that can be used to make alcoholic drinks.

In China, the city of Shaoxing is famous for its rice wines, produced using a *qu* made from wheat and known as 'yellow wines' because of their golden colour. There are different types of Shaoxing rice wine, ranging from dry to sweet; the medium-dry varieties are drunk most often, served

Opposite: Rice wine has been brewed in Japan, where it is known as *sake*, for centuries. This drawing by the Japanese artist Katsushika Hokusai, famed for his woodblock print series *Thirty-Six Views of Mount Fuji*, shows the labour involved in its production.

Katsushika Hokusai, *Three Men Brew Rice Wine on the Orders of Yi Di*, 1820s–40s. Japan. Ink on paper. H. 10.5 cm, W. 15.2 cm. 2020,3015.91. Purchase funded by the Theresia Gerda Buch Bequest, in memory of her parents Rudolf and Julie Buch, with support from Art Fund (with a contribution from the Wolfson Foundation).

Left: In Japan, *sake* is a drink rich in cultural significance, long offered to the gods. It is served at social occasions, including weddings and other celebrations. The pouring of *sake* for others from ewers, such as this one, is an act of polite hospitality.

Sake ewer, 1651–1700. Arita, Japan. Porcelain. H. 16.5 cm, Diam. 14.7 cm. Franks.1046. Donated by Sir Augustus Wollaston Franks.

lukewarm in small porcelain cups. Traditionally, rice wine is enjoyed on special occasions and celebrations. At Chinese weddings, it is customary for the bride and groom to each drink half a cup of wine, then exchange cups and drink the remaining half. It is also valued as a tonic, given to pregnant women and nursing mothers. Rice wine is an important ingredient in the Chinese kitchen, classically used to marinate fish, meat and chicken.

Sake (Japanese rice wine) is an important, traditional beverage in Japan; the process of making it has been refined over centuries. *Sake* is made from polished grains of rice, which are inoculated with an *Aspergillus oryza* mould culture called *koji*. The rice is polished to remove the bran (the brown outer layer), as retaining the bran would prevent the development of the desired fruity aroma. While table rice is polished to remove around 10 per cent of the bran, rice for *sake* has usually had 30 per cent of the grain polished away.

Sake has long been regarded as a special beverage, given as an offering at Shinto shrines and drunk on such special occasions as festivals, weddings and funerals. In Japanese mythology, the deity Susanoo-no-Mikoto used *sake* to get a monstrous serpent drunk and so defeat it.

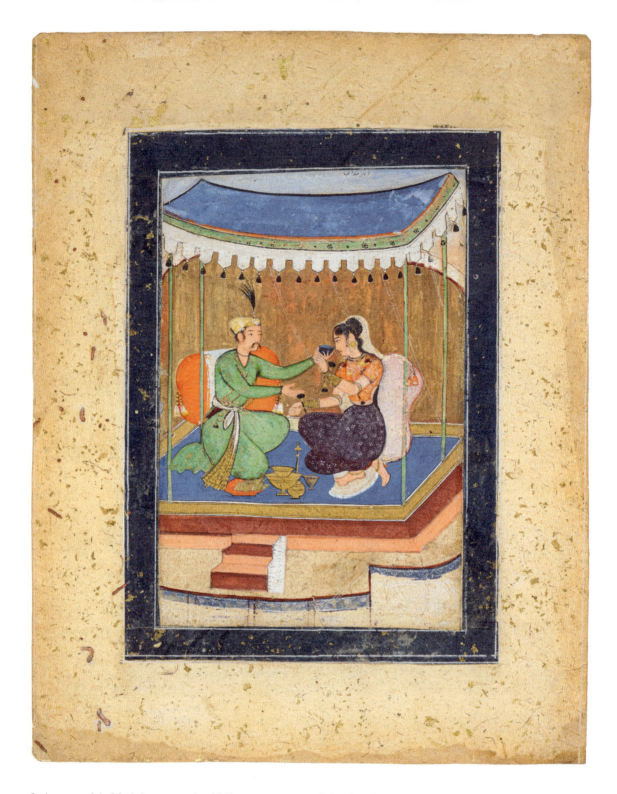

In the courts of the Mughal emperors, wine-drinking was customary until the reign of Aurangzeb (r. 1658–1707). In this image of recreational drinking, a man and a woman are seated under a canopy. The man offers a cup of wine to the woman, who bends her head to smell the proffered beverage.

Painting, *c.* 1610. India. Watercolour on paper. H. 26.4 cm, W. 20.7 cm. 1947,1011,0.1.

Above: Prohibition, forbidding the production, transport and sale of alcohol in the United States, had ended only a few years before John Sloan, known for his depictions of urban life, created this print. The gallery guests seem more interested in the cocktails than the art.

John Sloan, *A Thirst for Art*, 1939. USA. Etching on paper. H. 10 cm, W. 15.2 cm. 1965,1211.27. Donated by Helen Farr Sloan.

Left: The Tang poet Li Bai was famous not only for his poetry but also for his love of wine. Indeed, a number of his poems celebrate drinking and drunkenness. Here, the poet is shown in a characteristic pose, his wistful gaze focused on an empty wine jar.

Figure, 1662–1722. Jingdezhen, China. Glazed porcelain. H. 15 cm, W. 16 cm, D. 8 cm. Franks.500.+. Donated by Sir Augustus Wollaston Franks.

Above: Inns in Japan were traditionally places where food and alcohol could be enjoyed, with maids in constant attendance to offer drinks to guests. This comical print shows two travellers who have probably had a little too much *sake*.

Yanagawa Shigenobu, *Mariko, Two Ri from Okabe*, 1830s. Japan. Colour woodblock print on paper. H. 12 cm, W. 16.7 cm. 1906,1220,0.616.

Left: During the Qing dynasty in Imperial China, courtiers had to undertake a three-day period of abstinence from various activities – including the eating of meat, the drinking of alcohol and sexual intercourse – before the worshipping of ancestors, Heaven or other gods. To signal this abstention, pendant plaques such as this one were worn.

Abstinence plaque, c. 1800. Jingdezhen, China. Porcelain, enamel. H. 5.5 cm, W. 4.3 cm. Franks.573.+. Donated by Sir Augustus Wollaston Franks.

Left, top: In this scathing, satirical print, the artist William Hogarth portrays the social degradation caused by the over-consumption of gin by the poor in eighteenth-century London. The drink was nicknamed 'Mother's Ruin', and Hogarth shows a drunken mother carelessly letting her baby fall – presumably to its death.

William Hogarth, *Gin Lane*, 1751. Published in London, UK. Etching and engraving on paper. H. 37.4 cm, W. 31.8 cm. 1868,0822.1595. Bequeathed by Felix Slade.

Left, bottom: This dramatic depiction of a family brought to ruin through alcoholism was part of a series of prints commissioned by the Temperance reformer Joseph Adshead. The print's creator, artist George Cruikshank, had himself been a heavy drinker but joined the Temperance movement after taking the pledge to abstain.

George Cruikshank, *Cold, Misery, and Want, destroy their youngest Child: they console themselves with the Bottle*, 1847. Published in London, UK. Etching on paper. H. 25 cm, W. 35.5 cm. 1978,U.331. Bequeathed by Eliza Cruikshank.

Preserving and processing

The world of food is filled with examples of human ingenuity in transforming raw ingredients into foods that both keep and eat well. Historically, the starting point for preserving was the importance of finding a way of making perishable food keep better. Thus, for example, fresh milk and cream were turned into cheese and butter, both of which can be stored for longer. Similarly, precious fresh meat – often regarded as a luxury – was cured and turned into charcuterie products, including salamis and hams. In the quest to make raw ingredients edible and digestible, people have found ways of processing them. Perhaps the most well known is the grinding of hard, indigestible grains into flour from which to make bread, a vital staple.

Over the centuries, various ways of preserving food have been discovered and developed. The drying of such foods as fresh fruit or wild fungi, using the natural warmth of the sun or the heat from fire, is a basic, long-practised procedure. Smoking fresh fish or meat is another historic preserving method, one that imparts a distinctive flavour to the food. Fermentation is yet another ancient preserving technique, used to create foodstuffs like kimchi and sauerkraut.

Salt has long been used as an essential ingredient in many types of preserving, owing to its ability to draw out the moisture in food through the process of osmosis. The resulting dry, salty environment inhibits the growth of bacteria, which would otherwise spoil the food. Salting is therefore a key stage in many preserving processes, from pickling to cheese-making.

Sugar, similarly, draws out the moisture from foods through osmosis. With its sweet taste, sugar is often used to preserve fruit, by turning it into jam or sweetened fruit pastes (such as membrillo, Spanish quince paste), storing it in syrup or crystallizing it. Vinegar has been used for many years not just as a condiment but also as a preserving agent, the acetic acid contained in vinegar inhibiting the growth of spoilage bacteria. In many countries, one still finds a cycle of preserving rooted in the seasons, where abundant fresh produce – strawberries, mangoes, tomatoes – is transformed into jams, pickles and chutneys to be stored away for future consumption. Other, more recent methods of preserving food, which are widely used today, include canning and freezing.

In an age of refrigeration, the need to use traditional preserving methods has notably diminished. Strikingly, however, we still appreciate the flavours and textures of many preserved foods. The skills underlying traditional methods of fermenting, curing and smoking continue to be valued, with the resulting products finding a receptive audience in delicatessens and restaurant kitchens. Foods including Spain's Iberico ham, China's Nuodeng ham, Italy's Parmigiano Reggiano cheese, France's marrons glacés and artisan smoked salmon enjoy a luxurious status. In the West, an interest in gut health has seen a rise in popularity and availability of foods and drinks made using traditional fermentation processes, such as sourdough, kombucha and kefir.

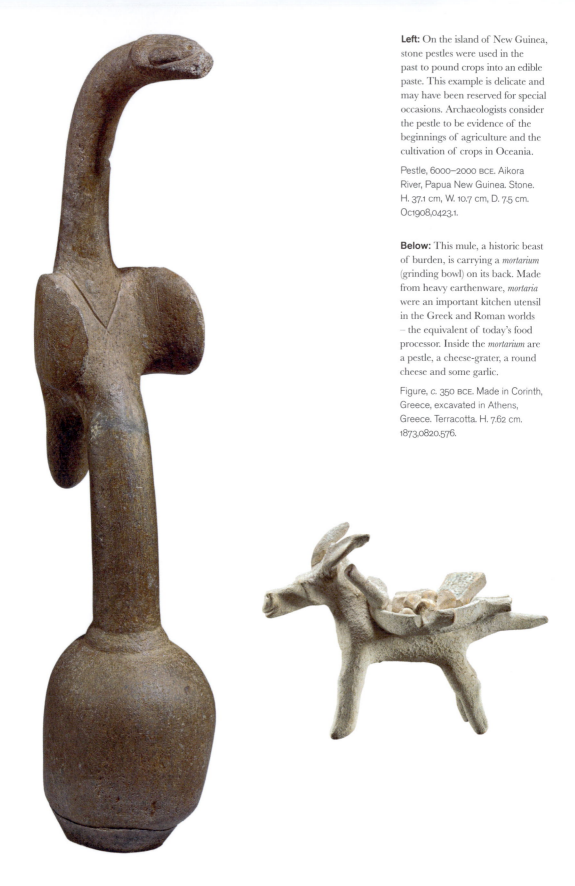

Left: On the island of New Guinea, stone pestles were used in the past to pound crops into an edible paste. This example is delicate and may have been reserved for special occasions. Archaeologists consider the pestle to be evidence of the beginnings of agriculture and the cultivation of crops in Oceania.

Pestle, 6000–2000 BCE. Aikora River, Papua New Guinea. Stone. H. 37.1 cm, W. 10.7 cm, D. 7.5 cm. Oc1908,0423.1.

Below: This mule, a historic beast of burden, is carrying a *mortarium* (grinding bowl) on its back. Made from heavy earthenware, *mortaria* were an important kitchen utensil in the Greek and Roman worlds – the equivalent of today's food processor. Inside the *mortarium* are a pestle, a cheese-grater, a round cheese and some garlic.

Figure, *c.* 350 BCE. Made in Corinth, Greece, excavated in Athens, Greece. Terracotta. H. 7.62 cm. 1873,0820.576.

Many of the key ingredients in Korean cuisine, such as kimchi and gochujang (chilli paste), are made by pickling and fermentation. Large earthenware jars called *onggi* have been used to store and ferment foodstuffs in Korea for millennia, with their microporous structure aiding the fermentation process.

Jar, 1875–1925. Korea. Earthenware. H. 113.8 cm, Diam. 63.7 cm (lid). 1990,1114.9.a-b.

SALT

Salt (sodium chloride), a simple inorganic mineral, plays a special part in the human diet. Biologically, saltiness is one of the five basic tastes recognized by receptors on our tongues. Saltiness – up to a point – is a flavour enjoyed and prized by humans, with salt widely used as a seasoning in food. More importantly, however, sodium chloride is a nutrient that is essential to the proper functioning of the human body. Our bodies do not produce it on their own, so it has to be found and consumed.

Naturally occurring salt is found in seawater, in brine springs and in underground, crystalline rock-salt deposits, created many years ago through the evaporation of ancient seas. Human beings have long found ways of obtaining salt, including through the power of sun and wind. Shallow pools of salt water were evaporated by the sun's heat and the drying effects of the wind, leaving residual salt crystals behind. The making of salt by means of natural solar evaporation is still practised to this day. Another way of producing salt was by boiling salt water to obtain the salt crystals; an early written record of salt production in China, dating to around 800 BCE, describes this method. For several centuries, humans have manually quarried rock salt from the earth, a laborious, often dangerous process. When large deposits of salt were found underground, huge salt mines were created to exploit this valuable resource. Among the world's historic salt mines are those at Hallstatt in Austria, Khewra in Pakistan and Wieliczka in Poland.

Salt blocks were one of the most widespread forms of currency in Ethiopia, with records showing that it was often preferred to other means of payment. Salt bars such as this one were used for barter or as small change, but they were also accepted as legal tender for the payment of taxes or fines.

Salt currency, before 1925. Ethiopia. Salt, leaf. H. 15.7 cm, W. 33.4 cm, D. 12.8 cm. Af1925,1017.1. Donated by Benjamin White.

Allowing dinner guests to add salt to their food, according to their preferences, required containers for the table. Wealthy households bought attractive salt pots and cellars made of luxurious materials, such as this late fifteenth-century Venetian example made from glass decorated with green and blue enamel and gold.

Salt cellar, c. 1480–1520. Venice, Italy. Glass, gold, enamel. H. 5.4 cm. S.366. Bequeathed by Felix Slade.

Salt is also important for its role in preserving food. It does this through osmosis, drawing out the moisture from such products as meat, fish and vegetables. This dehydrating process inhibits the growth of spoilage bacteria, which require the presence of water to thrive, and so helps preserve the foods. Salt also creates an environment in which harmless, flavour-enhancing, salt-resistant bacteria can thrive, playing a key part in making many of the processed foodstuffs we value. Salted foods, which can be stored and taken on long journeys, formed essential supplies for armies and navies.

For many years, salt was a highly valuable commodity, transported and traded over both land and water; the term 'salt road', used to describe historic trade routes, reflects its economic importance. The word 'salary' derives from the Latin *salarium*, the wages paid to Roman soldiers that included salt. Taxing salt was a lucrative source of income for governments around the world, and resistance to unpopular salt taxes in countries like France and India forms part of salt's history.

In the culinary world, one can find a variety of salts. Examples include Indian *kala namak* (black salt); Himalayan rock salt, tinted pink from trace minerals; and *fleur de sel* (flower of the salt), which enjoys a particular cachet. France is a notable producer of this last variety, created from the delicate crust of crystals carefully harvested from the surface of sea water sitting in shallow pools.

Vinegar occurs naturally when fermented plant juice, such as wine, turns sour through the action of bacteria, changing alcohol into acetic acid. Indeed, the word 'vinegar' comes from the French *vin aigre*, meaning 'sour wine'. Historically, vinegar has been prized for its preserving, medicinal and flavouring properties.

Edme Bouchardon, a vinegar seller, *c.* 1730s. France. Red chalk pasted on brown paper, within brown wash border. H. 23 cm, W. 17.9 cm. 1857,0613.761.

This Dutch delftware cruet set consists of two small, lidded bottles in a matching stand, one marked 'O' for *olio* (oil), the other 'A' for *aceto* (vinegar). Placed on the dining table, the set allowed guests to dress their food to taste, with the stand preventing any dribbles from staining fine linen tablecloths.

Cruet set, early 18th century. The Netherlands. Earthenware. H. 17.7 cm. 1927,0616.1.CR. Donated by J. W. Clarke.

Mustard, a condiment made from the seeds of the mustard plant, is widely appreciated for its enlivening, pungent piquancy. It was an important spice in Europe during the Middle Ages: it grew locally, and was therefore more affordable than exotic, imported spices. This Chinese mustard pot was made for the European market, and was found in the wreck of a Chinese junk bound for Batavia.

Mustard pot, *c.* 1643. Jingdezhen, China. Glazed porcelain. H. 4.6 cm. 1984,0303.9.

DAIRY

Like other mammals, humans begin life consuming milk, the nutritious fluid produced by female mammals to feed their young. Uniquely in the natural world, humans also consume milk from other mammals, such as cows, sheep, goats, camels, yaks and water buffalo. These ruminant (cud-chewing) animals have long been valued for their capacity to live on grass and give milk. This milk, and the dairy products made from it, have sustained people for millennia. However, only some individuals have the capacity to carry on drinking milk after infancy. Milk contains the milk sugar lactose (only found in milk), which requires the presence of lactase, a digestive enzyme, in the human digestive system to break it down successfully. Lactase levels decline in most people after weaning, and this lack of lactase leads to lactose intolerance. However, human populations with a long history of keeping dairy animals, like the pastoralists of east and west Africa and northern Europeans, retain lactase in their bodies and so can consume milk with no adverse effects.

Milk is rich in protein, sugars, fat, calcium and certain vitamins. It is also highly perishable, and over thousands of years people have found ways of preserving and transforming this prized liquid into dairy products. Certain characteristics of milk are thought to have played a part in the development

Dairy products – milk, ghee, butter – are important in Hindu stories and rituals. In the iconography of the Hindu god Krishna, he is often depicted as a small child either playing with or stealing a pat of butter. His childhood nickname was *makhan chor*, or 'butter thief'.

Figure of Balakrishna holding a pat of butter, 18th century. Maharashtra, India. Bronze. H. 6.4 cm. 1940,0716.281. Donated by Mrs A. G. Moor.

The milking of cows, sheep or goats and the making of dairy products was a task frequently carried out by women. The figure of the milkmaid was often represented as a young, comely woman, the picture of wholesome beauty and innocence.

George Shepheard, a milkmaid with a dog, 1815. UK. Graphite drawing on paper. H. 21.2 cm, W. 27 cm. 1902,1018.21.

of a dairy tradition. Milk's fat content, for example, means that milk set aside in a container will naturally see fat globules rise to the surface and form a layer, known as cream. This can be skimmed off and eaten in its own right. Butter is made simply by agitating cream (classically in a butter churn) until the butterfat clumps together, expelling a white liquid known as buttermilk.

A number of dairy products, yoghurt and cheese among them, are made using fermentation. Key to creating these products are the actions of a particular group of microbes known as lactic acid bacteria. These microbes consume the lactose found in milk and release lactic acid, causing the milk to sour. This souring process usefully inhibits the growth of other, undesirable bacteria. As milk sours it curdles, leading to the creation of curds and liquid whey. Milk also curdles, when such coagulants as lemon juice or rennet (a blend of enzymes found in the stomachs of young ruminants, including kids and calves) are added to it. One theory regarding the early origins of cheese-making is that milk carried on journeys in bags made from animal stomachs curdled in reaction to the rennet that was present, creating curds and whey and, it is thought, leading to the realization that milk could be transformed into cheese.

The nineteenth century saw the industrialization of dairy production in Europe and North America. One important step was the pasteurization of milk. Named after the French scientist Louis Pasteur, who pioneered the concept in the 1860s, pasteurization is a heat treatment that kills bacteria, including dangerous pathogens. The arrival of the railways meant that fresh milk could be transported from farms in the countryside to cities, where it was in high demand. In an era of refrigeration, consumers nowadays can choose from a diverse range of dairy products. Interest in these products is on the rise in East and Southeast Asia, with China now the world's second largest consumer of dairy foods.

Below: A Swiss cheese-maker welcomes visitors to his mountain chalet to taste his wares. The long tradition of cheese-making in the Alps, where, during late spring, when the snow melts, cattle are taken up into the mountains to graze on the flower-rich meadows found there, continues to this day.

Sigmund Freudenberger, *La Visite au Chalet* (The Visit to the Chalet), 1770–1801. Published in Bern, Switzerland. Etching with hand-colouring on paper. H. 20.7 cm, W. 26.8 cm. 1958,0712.1202. Bequeathed by Robert Wylie Lloyd.

Right: Hard cheeses are formed by shaping the curd produced by curdling milk and draining off the moisture. This Roman British bowl has holes in its base and sides to allow this drainage to occur. Once filled, the bowl was probably covered with a cloth and weighted in order to press the curds into a solid mass.

Cheese press, 1st–2nd century CE. Boxstead Farm, Kent, UK. Pottery. H. 6.6 cm, Diam. 20 cm. 1883,1213.424.

Historically, the ability to buy fresh milk was important for households in towns or cities without their own dairy animals. Common complaints, however, were that the milk was dirty or watered down by unscrupulous dairymen seeking to increase their profits.

Giovanni Antonio da Brescia, a milk-seller, 1510–20. Italy. Engraving on paper. H. 18.5 cm, W. 12.3 cm. 1845,0825.719.

OLIVE OIL

Hardy, slow-growing and long-lived, the evergreen olive tree (*Olea europaea*) was first cultivated in the eastern Mediterranean around 5,000 or 6,000 years ago, and is especially associated with the Mediterranean region. The tree is cultivated for its fruit, a fleshy drupe called an olive. Owing to the natural presence of a glucoside called oleuropein, olives are remarkably bitter and are therefore not eaten raw when freshly picked. Instead, they are preserved using a process that renders them palatable, transforming them into table olives.

Rather than for their eating properties, however, it is for their high fat content – extracted by pressing the fruit to release its oil – that olives have long been prized. Olive oil has historically been used as a fuel to light lamps, in medicine, in cosmetics and in cooking, with its versatility and the fact it can be stored and transported making it a valuable trading commodity. Significantly, it is from the Greek word for olive, *elaia*, that words for oil in other languages have been derived: *olio* in Italian, *huile* in French, and *oil* in English. Olive cultivation spread throughout the Mediterranean region, including to Crete and Greece, with the Etruscans credited with introducing it into Italy and the Phoenicians into the Iberian peninsula and North Africa. The olive was also important to the Romans, who spread olive cultivation within their empire. Much space is given to the subject of olive-growing in *De agri cultura*, Cato the Elder's treatise on farming, written in about 160 BCE.

To make olive oil, the olives are harvested from the trees both as they approach maturity but are still green, and when they mature and turn black. In the Mediterranean, this harvest occurs during the late autumn and early winter months. Olives were harvested by shaking and beating the tree with poles and collecting the fruits by hand; however, in larger-scale production,

The olive tree has been important in Greece for millennia. In Greek mythology, the two gods Poseidon and Athena competed for patronage of Athens. Athena gave the city the gift of an olive tree and won the competition. Here, she wears a helmet decorated with olive leaves.

Coin, 450–406 BCE. Minted in Athens, Greece. Silver. Diam. 2.1 cm, 17.2 g. 1947,0406.254.

Traditionally, olives were harvested by hand and by pole beating the tree, a time-consuming, laborious process. Today, olives are still harvested this way, but mechanical means are also used. The gentle shaking of the tree or the combing of its branches to dislodge the fruit can now be carried out by machine.

Amphora, c. 520 BCE. Made in Athens, Greece, excavated at Vulci, Italy. Pottery. H. 40.6 cm. 1837,0609.42.

mechanical tree-shakers are used to dislodge the olives. The collected olives are then crushed into a paste, a process historically carried out using heavy millstones. The oil is obtained from this paste, usually using centrifugal force to separate the oil from the water.

Today, olives are still grown largely for their oil; however, in an age of electricity, the oil is valued as a culinary product rather than as a fuel. Indeed, olive oil is seen as a characteristic ingredient of Mediterranean cuisine. It is widely used in the kitchen, lending its distinctive flavour to salad dressings and such foodstuffs and dishes as Italy's focaccia bread, France's brandade and Spain's tortilla. Olive oil for consumption is categorized and described in a number of ways. 'Virgin olive oil' is the term used for olive oil obtained directly by pressing olives with an oleic acid content of less than 3 per cent. 'Extra virgin olive oil' must have an oleic acid content of less than 0.8 per cent; the low oleic acidity is a sign of quality. 'Olive oil' is made by blending refined olive oil – obtained using heat, pressure and chemicals – with a quantity of virgin oil. Spain is the world's largest producer of virgin olive oil, but olives are now grown in countries around the world, including Morocco, Australia and China.

Portuguese traders reached Africa's west coast in the mid-fifteenth century, marking the start of regular contact and trade. Traditionally, ivory carvings were produced only for the royal court in Benin; however, the ruling Oba (king) allowed certain ivory carvings, such as this salt cellar, to be made for European visitors.

Salt cellar, c. 1525–1600. Possibly made by Edo people in Nigeria. Ivory. H. 29.3 cm, W. 11 cm. Af1878,1101.48.a-c.

Left: According to the inscription at the bottom of this drawing, its subject was employed to look after the cellar and larder of an Italian cardinal. In the pre-refrigeration era, keeping a larder well stocked with stores of food was an important task, and much work was done during the summer and autumn, gathering and preserving provisions for the lean winter months ahead.

Pier Leone Ghezzi, caricature of Giovan Battista Griscio, 1745. Italy. Pen and brown ink over black chalk on paper. H. 32.4 cm, W. 22.4 cm. 1859,0806.246.

Below: Drying fish is an ancient, basic way of preserving a valuable fresh food. Dried fish, as depicted in this netsuke, are an important ingredient in Japanese cuisine. Umami-rich *katsuobushi*, made from dried, smoked and fermented bonito flesh, is a typical ingredient in *dashi*, Japanese stock.

Netsuke, early 18th century. Japan. Wood, lacquer, mother-of-pearl, fish skin. L. 11 cm. F.1078. Donated by Sir Augustus Wollaston Franks.

The drought-tolerant root vegetable cassava is an important staple in western Africa. Cassava, as well as other starchy tubers such as yams, is often made into a dish called fufu. To make fufu, cassava is boiled and then pounded into a smooth paste – as the mother in this model group is doing.

Model group, early 20th century. Made by Bamum people, Cameroon. Brass, wood. H. 14.5 cm, W. 5 cm, D. 9 cm. 2014,2011.282. Donated by Leila Ingrams.

Right: This agricultural scene shows the work that went into providing bread for the table in the pre-industrial era. In the background, fields are being ploughed; meanwhile, in the foreground, a farmer laboriously grinds grain while a woman carefully tends the loaves baking in an oven.

Monogrammist CA, a farmer and his wife, 1502–20. Germany. Woodcut on paper. H. 11.4 cm, W. 14.5 cm. 1877,0512.868. Donated by P. Abraham, Esq.

Above: Grinding grain into flour is arduous work, and both water and wind power have been harnessed to help make the task easier. In Britain, watermills were a prime means of milling for centuries. This print shows a bag of flour being filled inside a water mill, while outside more are being loaded onto a cart.

Joseph Mallord William Turner, *Pembury Mill, Kent*, 1808. Published in London, UK. Mezzotint and etching on paper. H. 20.9 cm, W. 18.9 cm. 1869,1109.24.

TEA

After water, tea is the most widely consumed beverage in the world. A non-alcoholic drink of great cultural and economic significance, it is made by infusing the leaves of the plant *Camellia sinensis* in water. A key part of tea's importance is that it contains caffeine, a behaviour-modifying alkaloid valued for its stimulating effects on the human body.

Tea is made by processing freshly picked tea leaves, with 4 to 5 kilograms of fresh leaves required to make 1 kilogram of processed tea. As soon as the leaves are picked, they begin to wilt, with tea producers using this natural withering as part of the tea-making process. Next comes oxidation, a key stage, with different oxidization levels a major factor in creating different types of tea. Green teas, for example, are oxidized at only around 5 per cent; in contrast, black teas are oxidized at 70 per cent or upwards, an effect created by rolling or cutting up the leaves to expose them to oxygen. The leaves are then heat-treated to halt any further oxidation and de-enzyme them. They may then be rolled and dried to reduce the moisture content to 5 per cent or less, which stabilizes the tea and allows it to be stored.

Camellia sinensis is native to the highlands between India and China. Tea itself originates from China, where it has been drunk for centuries. In one apocryphal story, the discovery of tea is credited to Shennong (see page 66), the second of China's legendary emperors whose name translates as 'Divine Farmer'. Another legend attributes the discovery of tea to a Buddhist monk who cut off his eyelids as penance for falling asleep while meditating and

Depicting pine, bamboo and plum trees, the design on this teapot is known as the 'Three Friends of Winter'. The long-lived, evergreen pine tree represents stability, the bamboo symbolizes the Confucian gentleman-scholar, who bends without breaking, while the plum, the first to flower in the New Year, stands for purity and leadership.

Teapot, 1723–35. Jingdezhen, China. Porcelain, enamel. H. 13.7 cm, W. 10.7 cm. PDF,A.798. On loan to the British Museum from the Sir Percival David Collection.

In Britain, tea-drinking is often associated with the light meal known as afternoon tea. The custom is popularly credited to the Duchess of Bedford, who, in around 1840, requested that tea, bread and cake be served to her in the late afternoon.

Helen Binyon, *The Tea-Party*, c. 1930–40. UK. Engraving on oriental paper. H. 13.8 cm, W. 17.2 cm. 1985,0119.38. Donated by Margaret Higgens.

threw them to the ground. From these eyelids sprang two tea bushes. Buddhist monks were indeed noted for their high tea consumption, with the beverage's wakeful properties prized as an aid to conscious meditation. By the start of the Tang dynasty, tea drinking was an accepted and refined custom in Chinese society.

From the early sixteenth century onwards, Europeans, initially the Portuguese and the Dutch, began trading with China, purchasing such precious goods as silk, porcelain and tea, and acquired a taste for tea drinking. The British desire for tea saw the British East India Company import large amounts of tea from China, for which the Chinese were paid in precious metals. Britain sought to find an alternative to China's lucrative monopoly on tea production, and in 1834 set up a Tea Committee to create a tea industry in India. The plant hunter Robert Fortune and others were employed to travel around China and smuggle out tea plants and seeds. The British introduced the Chinese tea varietal *Camellia sinensis* var. *sinensis* to India, where it did well in Darjeeling. It was, however, India's native varietal, *Camellia sinensis* var. *Assamica*, that suited the climate of Assam; it also thrived in Sri Lanka, Malawi and Kenya, where the British started tea plantations during the nineteenth and twentieth centuries. Today, the tea plant is grown on every continent except for Antarctica, and tea is both widely available and affordable.

The onset of direct trade between China and the United States in the mid-1780s increased the market for Chinese export lacquers, decorative articles made of wood and coated in lacquer. Small items included tea caddies, designed to keep the tea safe and dry. The majority of caddies were equipped with removable pewter liners for different varieties of tea.

Tea chest, 1810–25. Fujian, China. Wood, lacquer, pewter. H. 15.5 cm, W. 26.5 cm, D. 38.5 cm. 2016,3064.1. Funded by Brooke Sewell Permanent Fund.

This flower-shaped pewter box contains six *famille rose* porcelain tea caddies. The covers of the caddies are inscribed in gold with the names of different teas. The four black teas named – 'Congou' (Congo), 'Gobee' (Bohea), 'Sauchon' (Souchong) and 'Pecko' (Pekoe) – were the main kinds exported from China.

Box of tea caddies, c. 1760–80. China. Porcelain, pewter. H. 11.8 cm (box), H. 11 cm (caddies). Franks.1688. Donated by Sir Augustus Wollaston Franks.

Japanese matcha tea is traditionally made in a *chawan* (tea bowl) by whisking finely ground green tea in water using a springy bamboo whisk called a *chasen*. This dainty netsuke, made from stained ivory, cleverly imitates a *chasen* inside a Raku-ware tea bowl.

Netsuke, late 19th century. Japan. Ivory. H. 2.2 cm, W. 3.70 cm. F.1122. Donated by Sir Augustus Wollaston Franks.

Cooking

Cooking – the transformation of raw foods through the application of heat – is a uniquely human activity. This everyday practice, something found in every known society, has played an important part in human history.

Cooking is historically related to the ability to manage fire. Fire has many uses, providing not only light and warmth but also, significantly, the capacity to cook food. Exactly when humans first started cooking is not known. One theory proposes that roasting meat might date back as far as 1.8 million years ago. Examination of fish remains at the Gesher Benot Ya'aqov archaeological site in Israel suggests that cooking took place here around 780,000 years ago.

What is more widely agreed, however, is that eating cooked food had a major impact on the evolution of the human body. Cooking food softens it: humans, compared to other primates, have small jaws and small, weak teeth, strong enough to eat cooked food but inadequate for eating tough, raw food. Cooked food is high in calories, which provide energy for the body, and can be digested far more easily than raw food, which allowed for human brains to grow and human guts to shrink. Although only about 2.5 per cent of our body weight, the human brain requires a lot of energy, which calorie-packed, easily digestible cooked food can deliver. Cooking also made food safer to eat by killing pathogens. Many raw plants contain toxins and substances that the human body is unable to digest. Cooking often neutralizes these unwanted elements, allowing humans to consume and digest them.

Long before the advent of agriculture, people were gathering tiny, hard, wild seeds and cooking them. The ability to cook meant that many more foods could be eaten, thereby extending the range of possible ingredients. In addition, cooking makes food more enticing, adding flavours and textures that are appealing to humans and other predators. When such foodstuffs as meat are browned, for example, the Maillard reaction occurs (named for the French chemist Louis Camille Maillard, who first described it in 1912), producing savoury aromas and agreeable flavours.

The advent of cooking is thought to have encouraged socializing around food. Whereas gathered raw ingredients could be eaten where they had been found, cooking them required the creation of a fire using precious fuel. From campfires to kitchen hearths, fires have long been focal points around which people have assembled. Over time, societies became shaped by mealtimes, set points in the day when food was consumed with others. Cooking methods have developed over the centuries, from cooking over fires, using hot-stones and pits, to the more recent use of microwave technology. Cooking is enjoyed by some, seen as a chore by others; either way, it remains an integral part of human life.

Right, top: This striking *mizusashi*, a water-container used for the Japanese tea ceremony, is a converted cooking pot. Dating back to the Jomon period (around 14,000–300 BCE), the pot is made of coiled, hand-moulded, low-fired red pottery. Many centuries later, its interior was lacquered in gold, and a lacquered, wooden lid (not shown) was added.

Water jar, 5000 BCE, gold lacquer interior decoration, early 19th century. Japan. Pottery, wood, lacquer, gold. H. 20 cm, Diam. 17 cm. OA+.20.

Right, bottom: The village of Babessi in the Cameroonian Grasslands was long noted for the quality of its pots. Traditionally made by women, Babessi pots were used in a number of ways: as daily cookware, as storage containers, or for the making of medicine. Cooking pots, such as this example, were usually decorated in a relatively simple manner.

Cooking pot, 1994. Babessi, Cameroon. Pottery. H. 27.8 cm, W. 29.6 cm, D. 29.7 cm. Af1994,08.19.

Below: Cooks have been using cast-iron pots for centuries. In 1960, the celebrated Finnish designer Timo Sarpaneva reinvented the form for the modern kitchen, giving it a practical, detachable wooden handle for removing the lid from the hot pan. Sarpaneva's design has been in production ever since.

Cooking pot, 1960. Finland. Iron, teak. H. 16.5 cm, W. 23.5 cm. 2014,8024.148.a-c. Anonymous donation.

Right: Featuring sea creatures and intertwining vine and ivy leaves, the superb decoration on this small, bronze pan or skillet – used for frying or sauce preparation – suggests it was also presented at table. It is a rare piece and carries the name of its Roman British or Gallic maker, Boduogenus.

Skillet, 2nd century CE. Prickwillow, UK. Copper alloy. Diam. 16.5 cm, L. 15 cm (handle). 1893,0618.14.

SOUP

Soup – a liquid food made by boiling or simmering – is a remarkably versatile dish, ranging in nature from the frugal to the luxurious. Part of its flexibility is that it can be made from a wide variety of ingredients, including vegetables, meat, seafood and fruit. The consumption of soup is so widespread that tableware exists specifically for its serving and eating: lidded tureens from which to serve it at the table, soup ladles, soup bowls and soup spoons. Soup can also be found in folklore. In the traditional European folk tale 'Stone Soup', a hungry traveller ingeniously persuades his ungenerous hosts to add meaty bones and vegetables to a soup he says he is making only from a 'magic' stone, gradually transforming it into a hearty meal.

The fact that soup can be made from simple, affordable ingredients – water, pulses and vegetables, for example – means it has long been seen as offering a thrifty, warming meal for those on low incomes, as witnessed by the existence of soup kitchens. At the other end of the scale, soups can be made with the most costly ingredients. In Chinese cuisine, bird's nest soup and shark's fin soup were traditionally served at banquets, with their rare, hard-to-source ingredients adding a certain cachet, as well as a particular texture, to the soups. Both dishes continue to be regarded as luxuries, although in 2013 the Chinese government banned the serving of shark's fin soup at official banquets as part of an anti-corruption drive. In eighteenth- and nineteenth-century Britain, the serving at dinner parties of turtle soup, made using real turtles from the West Indies, was an indication of the host's social status. Those who couldn't afford to use real turtle served mock turtle soup – made from calf's head, which has a similar texture to turtle – instead.

Japanese soup bowls are typically lidded, for the practical purpose of keeping the soup hot. Produced in Arita, a venerable hub of Japanese porcelain production, this elegant soup bowl is made from eggshell porcelain.

Lidded soup bowl, 1870–85, Arita, Japan. Porcelain. H. 7.8 cm, Diam. 13.2 cm. Franks.1238.A.+. Donated by Sir Augustus Wollaston Franks.

Soup kitchens are places offering free food, traditionally soup and bread, to those who are homeless or destitute. They have a long history in many societies, and their establishment was often motivated by religious, charitable principles of giving to the needy.

William Strang, *The Soup Kitchen*, 1889. UK. Etching with sandpaper tone on paper. H. 30.1 cm, W. 25.4 cm. 1953,0509.112. Donated by Art Fund (as NACF).

Soup occupies a special place in Chinese cuisine, where it falls into two broad categories: *tang*, a light broth, and *geng*, a thicker, almost stew-like soup. *Tang* is eaten at almost every meal, sometimes serving the role of a drink. *Geng* was a very important dish historically, mentioned in the ancient *Book of Rites*. Both dishes can be made either from everyday ingredients, such as vegetables, or from luxurious ones, such as game. Chinese soups were also often considered curative and healing, made using medicinal herbs and vegetables. The idea of soup being an excellent restorative – 'invalid food' – is one found in a number of cultures, with chicken soup, for example, nicknamed 'Jewish penicillin'.

The starting point for most soups is a stock. Stock can be made in a variety of ways, using meat or poultry bones, herbs, aromatics, vegetables or dried mushrooms as the base. In Japanese cuisine, a basic stock known as *dashi* is made using dried seaweed, dried bonito flakes and water. The intense flavours from the preserved components mean it requires infusing only for a few minutes. *Dashi* is the base for many dishes, including miso soup. In French cuisine, veal stock is made by simmering veal bones and vegetables for several hours. This stock, in a reduced form to intensify its flavour, also provides the base for some classic French sauces. Nowadays, stock cubes and powders have replaced traditional stocks in many kitchens, offering a quick starting point for soup-making.

Below, top: In the first millennium BCE, flesh-hooks were used to remove meat from cauldrons. Many are elaborately decorated, suggesting they were associated with socially important feasts. The Dunaverney flesh-hook has a wooden shaft encased in copper-alloy bands with cast swans facing ravens along its length.

Flesh-hook, 950–750 BCE. Dunaverney, Northern Ireland. Copper alloy, oak. L. 70 cm (in mount). 1856,1222.1.

Below, bottom: Cooking a one-pot meal for family and friends was an important part of social life in the first millennium BCE. The Battersea cauldron is typical of the large, bronze vessels used for preparing a communal meal enjoyed by company sitting around the fire and dipping into the pot with flesh-hooks or ladles.

Cauldron, *c.* 800–600 BCE. Thames River, Battersea, UK. Copper alloy. H. 40.5 cm, Diam. 56 cm. 1861,0309.1.

Opposite: Copper is a ductile metal with a long history of use. This print playfully depicts a coppersmith with a body composed of cauldrons, pans and colanders. Thanks to the metal's capacity to heat up evenly and quickly, copper pans remain popular today.

Gerard Valck, *Habit de chaudronnier* (Coppersmith's Clothing), 1695–1720. The Netherlands. Etching and engraving on paper. H. 25.8 cm, W. 17.4 cm. I,7.195.

Habit de Chaudronnier

Rice is an important foodstuff in Southeast Asian cuisine. It is often cooked in coconut milk for richness, with pandan leaves added for fragrance. A popular and long-standing way of cooking rice is to steam it. This nineteenth-century Malaysian rice steamer is made from local plant materials.

Rice steamer, mid-19th century. Straits Settlements, Southeast Asia. Cane, leaf. H. 35 cm, Diam. 22.2 cm. As1886,1213.75. Donated by Government of Straits Settlements

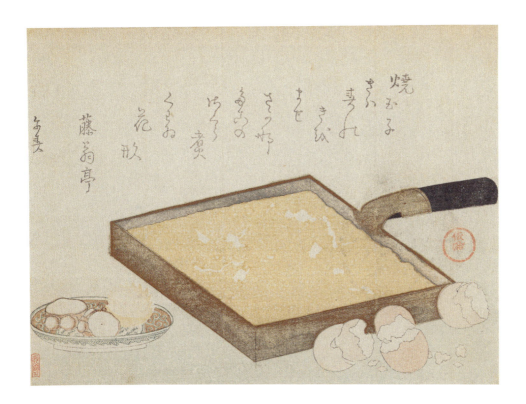

Above: Japanese omelette pans are traditionally rectangular or square, as can be seen in this woodblock print. They are used to make *tamago-yaki*, a Japanese rolled omelette eaten from bento boxes or used in sushi, with the pan's form allowing for neatly shaped rolls.

Kubo Shunman, omelette frying pan and eggshells, 1790–1810. Edo, Japan. Colour woodblock print on paper. H. 14.1 cm, W. 18.9 cm. 2006,0322,0.1.17. Purchase funded by the Brooke Sewell Bequest.

Below: Among the Indigenous Peoples of North America, tightly woven baskets made using the coiled or twined techniques, such as this Karuk example, could be used for cooking. The plant fibres swell when they become wet, making them watertight. Stews or soups were cooked by adding fire-heated stones to the liquid contents of the basket.

Basket, before 1949. Made by Karuk, also known as Karok, California, USA. Bear grass, spruce root, willow root, hazel wood, willow, maidenhair fern fibre (?). Diam. 20.9 cm. Am1949,02.27.

BREAD

Bread is a foodstuff that is at once basic and remarkable. Long seen as fundamental to sustaining life, bread's historic importance is reflected in its cultural and social significance. It has special symbolic values in Judaism, Christianity and Islam, and is rich in folkloric and superstitious associations. Bread also has political and social import. Throughout history, rulers and governments have understood that, in order to prevent social unrest, their citizens must have enough bread to eat – as reflected in the Roman poet Juvenal's famous quip, 'Give them bread and circuses and they never revolt.'

The history of bread is closely linked to the human capacity to grow and mill cereals. The earliest breads were flat breads, made typically from a paste of ground grain and water and cooked on a flat stone on a fire. Flat breads are still made and eaten today in many parts of the world: the Mexican tortilla, the Middle Eastern lavash, the Indian roti. The flour for bread is produced by grinding grain, laborious work when done by hand with a pestle and mortar or a saddle quern. Over the centuries, mills were developed that harnessed the power of water and wind to effectively grind grain into fine flour. A significant advance in milling occurred in Switzerland in 1834 when the roller mill was used. The roller mill's capacity to break open wheat berries – the husked, whole wheat grains – enabled white flour to be produced efficiently, making it far more affordable.

The earliest evidence of leavened breads comes from ancient Egypt. The Egyptians also made beer – another fermented grain product – and the production of beer and bread are linked. Given Egypt's warm climate, initially, leavening may well have occurred naturally, when yeast spores, widely present in the atmosphere, settled on a portion of grain paste and

Composed of woven fibre, this *masob* is a special tray-cum-table from which to eat injera, Ethiopia's fermented flatbread, made from teff flour. The injera is placed on the tray before cooked foods are mounded on top. Diners then scoop up the food using pieces of injera.

Tray table, 20th century. Made by Amhara people, Ethiopia. Grass, skin, fibre. H. 75.5 cm, W. 67.5 cm, D. 69.3 cm. Af1971,20.1.a.

Left, top: Bread was a staple food in ancient Egypt, made from grains including barley and emmer wheat; preserved loaves of bread have been found in archaeological excavations. This model group depicts two figures, one tending a fire, the other kneading dough or grinding grain.

Model group, late Old Kingdom to early First Intermediate Period, c. 2300–2100 BCE. Asyut, Egypt. Wood. H. 23 cm, W. 42.5 cm, D. 9 cm. EA 45197.

Left, bottom: The remains of more than thirty bakeries have been found at Pompeii, complete with sizeable ovens; in one of these, a carbonized loaf of bread was discovered. There were also mills for grinding grain into flour for baking, worked by such draught animals as donkeys.

William Bernard Cooke, John Murray and Bartolomeo Pinelli, *Interior of a Bakers Shop*, 1818. Published in London, UK. Etching, with some engraving, on chine collé paper. H. 19.7 cm, W. 28.8 cm. 1879,0014.237.

began fermenting the dough. It was realized that barm, the frothy, yeasty foam that forms on the surface of beer as it ferments, could be used as a leavening agent. The same yeast (*Saccharomyces cerevisiae*) is widely used in both baking and brewing. Lactic fermentation is key to making sourdough bread, with the action of the lactic acid bacteria creating a distinctive sour tang. Reserving a portion of fermenting dough, known as a levain, to mix into a new batch of dough to leaven it, has long been a common baking practice. Raised breads were cooked in covered ovens, rather than on bake stones.

Baking became a profession in its own right, with bakers recorded in ancient Egypt, and bakers' guilds, dating from around 150 BCE, found in Rome. The industrialization of bread-making took place in the nineteenth and twentieth centuries. In 1961, what is known as the Chorleywood bread process was developed by a baking research station in Britain. This process considerably sped up the development of dough (historically a very time-consuming stage of bread-making) through the use of additives and intense mechanical agitation. The majority of industrially produced bread made in Britain today is baked using the Chorleywood method.

In this print, a French cook is satirically portrayed as a 'macaroni', a pejorative term for a man of extravagant, modish fashion. The bestselling, eighteenth-century cookbook author Hannah Glasse complained about the extravagant ways of French cooks in the kitchen.

A Macaroni French Cook, 1772. UK. Etching on paper. H. 23.8 cm, W. 16.6 cm. 1866,1208.890.

Right: The French painter and printmaker Édouard Vuillard was known as an *intimiste*, for his many works portraying scenes of domestic life. Vuillard depicted women sewing or cooking, carrying out the everyday tasks involved in running a household. This kitchen scene conveys a sense of calm orderliness.

Édouard Vuillard, *La Cuisinière* (The Cook), 1899. Published in Paris, France. Colour lithograph, printed on china paper. H. 35 cm, W. 27 cm. 1949,0411.3604. Bequeathed by Campbell Dodgson.

Above: The roasting of meat over an open fire required attention and the constant turning of a spit. The demanding task was given to servant boys and, for centuries, to turnspit dogs, which ran inside a wheel to power the spit. Here, Thomas Bewick, fancifully, shows a monkey basting roasting meat.

Thomas Bewick, illustration for *History of British Birds*, 1800. UK. Wood engraving on paper. H. 5.1 cm, W. 6.2 cm. 1860,0811.314.

Right, top: In an age of labour-saving devices, it is worth remembering the sheer hard work that has historically gone into preparing and cooking food. On this west African gold weight, two female figures are shown standing by a mortar, each pounding an unknown substance with a tall pestle – a method of food preparation still used in African communities today.

Gold weight, 18th–19th century. Made by Akan people, Ghana. Brass. H. 6.9 cm, W. 3 cm, D. 5.6 cm. Af1878,1228.5. Donated by Major F. J. Sidney Parry.

Right, bottom: Here, a Roman servant, possibly an enslaved man, is preparing food in a *mortarium*, a heavy bowl in which ingredients were ground and mixed. The fact that he is rubbing his eyes suggests that he was preparing raw onions, which, when cut, produce a chemical that can make our eyes smart and water.

Figure, 2nd century CE. Egypt. Terracotta. L. 6.5 cm. 1926,0930.17. Donated by Henry Hunter Calvert.

Left: This busy kitchen scene, with servants fetching, carrying and preparing ingredients, conveys the amount of work required to feed a great house. In the foreground, an opportunistic cat takes advantage of the bustle to steal a fish.

Luca Giordano, kitchen scene, c. 1680. Italy. Pen and brown ink, grey-brown wash, over black chalk on paper. H. 32.4 cm, W. 44.8 cm. 1950,1111.41. Purchased from Colnaghi, funded by H. L. Florence Fund.

Above: Spring Festival, or Chinese New Year, based on the lunisolar calendar, is the most important festival in China, with families gathering to mark it together with a New Year's Eve dinner. Traditionally, certain dishes are eaten during the celebration, many of them symbolizing auspicious things, such as money bag-shaped dumplings for wealth and long noodles for longevity.

Xinnian duo jiqing, Hejia le anran (Let New Year bring good fortune and joy and the whole family be happy and peaceful), 1801–2000. Printed in Yangliuqing, China. Woodblock print on paper. H. 58.5 cm, W. 97 cm. 1982,1217,0.202.

KITCHENS

While the kitchen – the place where food is prepared and cooked – has changed and evolved over the centuries, it has retained its core, practical function.

The capacity to cook food by heating it is fundamental to the kitchen. For centuries, a fire in an open hearth was the place where food was cooked. Roasting meat was done on a spit in the radiant heat of an open fire. The spit had to be turned continuously to avoid the meat burning or drying out, a time-consuming and laborious task. In Britain, where spit-roasting was a popular cooking method, ingenious devices were constructed to carry out this kitchen chore, among them spits turned by dog wheels, weight jacks or clockwork jacks.

In such large, wealthy establishments as royal palaces and country houses, where cooking had to be done on a large scale, kitchens, staffed by teams of servants, were correspondingly sizeable affairs. In Europe, in addition to the main kitchen, there was often a range of rooms, each with its own culinary function: larders and pantries in which to store ingredients, a scullery for washing and scouring pots and pans, a dairy for butter-making, a bakery with bread ovens.

In China, images of Zaojun, the kitchen god, were placed above stoves each year so that he could observe the happenings in the home. At New Year, to make way for the new images, the old ones were burned and the god sent to report to the Jade Emperor, the Daoist ruler of Heaven. His testimony regarding the family's behaviour decided their fortunes over the year ahead.

New Year calendar with the kitchen god Zaojun and his wife, 1873. Printed in Yangliuqing, China, found in Weixian, China. Woodblock print on paper. H. 31.4 cm, W. 21.6 cm. 1954,1113,0.5. Donated by Mrs R. E. A. Hughes-Jones.

Discoveries made in Britain during the Industrial Revolution enabled cast iron to be produced more affordably and efficiently. In British kitchens, open fireplaces were gradually replaced by kitchen ranges, made using cast iron. The grandly named Panklibanon in London's West End was a showroom for ironwork items, including stove grates.

John Harris the Younger, *The Panklibanon Show Room, and Stove Grate Manufactory*, 1847. UK. Etching and aquatint on paper. H. 32.4 cm, W. 25.5 cm. 1850,0112.47. Donated by John Harris the Younger.

Cooking over an open fire in Europe gradually gave way to cooking on an enclosed range. The scientist and inventor Benjamin Thompson, Count Rumford, is credited with inventing what became known as the Rumford range in the late eighteenth century. Instead of an open fire, which lost heat and created an uncomfortably hot, smoky environment, Rumford's invention consisted of a number of small, enclosed fires, with smoke carried away into the chimney. Initially, however, his stove was seen as too innovative and failed to catch on. It was later, during the nineteenth century, that range cookers became popular in domestic homes. Another important kitchen innovation during the same period was the use of gas instead of coal to fuel cookers. Gas was used to light homes, but not to cook over. The French-born chef Alexis Soyer was an early champion of gas cooking, installing cutting-edge gas cookers – free of coal and smoke and with controllable flames – in 1840 in his splendid kitchens at the Reform Club in London. The ease and convenience of cooking over gas saw this new kitchen fuel become the norm.

Kitchens manned by servants were often utilitarian places, tucked away in basements or housed outside the main house. During the twentieth century, however, the domestic kitchen became a workspace used by those who lived in the home rather than their servants. Fitted streamlined kitchens became the norm. The same century is also marked by a number of labour-saving gadgets designed to make cooking quicker and more convenient: fridges, freezers, microwaves, dishwashers, food processors, pressure cookers. Many of the food preparation, processing and preservation tasks previously carried out in kitchens are now done by outside manufacturers. In some countries, the idea of the kitchen as a social space – somewhere in which to both eat and cook – has become well established.

Above: George Scharf's painting of his own kitchen shows a noticeably tidy room. A maid holds a plate bearing a joint of meat. Behind her, a large Welsh dresser sports an impressive display of neatly arranged tableware, pots and pans.

George Scharf, the artist's kitchen, 1846. UK/Germany. Watercolour on paper. H. 24 cm, W. 37.6 cm. 1862,0614.80.

Left: The Flemish artist David Teniers the Younger, whose painting this print is based on, often depicted kitchen scenes. Here, a cook tends to something on the fireplace while two men look on. In the foreground, a man sits shelling mussels, a popular Low Countries food enjoyed to this day in Belgium.

Juan Antonio López, *Una Cocina* (A Kitchen), c. 1826–32. Printed in Madrid, Spain. Lithograph on chine collé paper. H. 30.8 cm, W. 44 cm. 1858,0417.1090.

Left: There is a sense of prosperous abundance to this kitchen scene. An artistically arranged pile of game birds and animals, including a hare or rabbit, fills a table. Two cooks can also be seen, hard at work; the one in the foreground is preparing oysters.

Frans Snyders, kitchen scene, c. 1594–1605. The Netherlands. Pen and brown ink with brown wash, over charcoal on paper. H. 23.3 cm, W. 42.7 cm. T,14.11. Bequeathed by William Fawkener.

Above: This Edo-period print shows the interior of Chojiya, an exclusive house of pleasure in the government-licensed Yoshiwara quarter of Tokyo. To the right, cooks and servants are busy preparing food in the kitchen area. On the left, a party is being held for a wealthy client.

Torii Kiyonaga, *Chojiya at Edo-cho ni-chome in Shin-Yoshiwara*, 1780s. Japan. Colour woodblock print on paper. H. 35 cm, W. 51 cm. 1908,0616,0.158.

Eating in

The domestic space plays a special part in shaping our relationship with food and sustaining culinary knowledge. Our homes are where we first encounter solid food as we are weaned, discovering the foodstuffs and flavours we like and dislike. They are the places where, as children, we are taught how to use such utensils as knives, forks, spoons or chopsticks, and where we learn the manners and good behaviour required when eating with other people, including the sharing of food. Many societies emphasize the importance of regular family meals in the home – occasions on which different generations can gather together around a table to eat, drink and talk. In an atomized age, these shared meals are seen as valuable, connective experiences.

Home cooking is often practical and thrifty, based on the realities of feeding a family economically. It is also seen as a source of comfort and reassurance, a tangible expression of affection. The process of cooking allows the home cook to be creative in the kitchen, adding their own touches with regards to ingredients, flavourings and cooking methods that make even a classic recipe their own. Frequently, family recipes are closely guarded secrets, shared only with near relatives. Some families possess treasured recipes that have been passed down through the generations, usually from grandmother to daughter to granddaughter, since, historically, home cooking has been very much a female occupation.

The food we first encounter as children has the capacity to trigger memories. There are biological reasons for this phenomenon. Our sense of smell is key to our ability to taste flavours. Aroma messages are processed by olfactory nerves that connect to the amygdala, the area of our brains that is involved in our emotional responses, including pleasure and fear. The amygdala is located close to the hippocampus, which creates memories from experiences. It is this power – of taste and smell – that the French novelist Marcel Proust evoked in the famous passage in his book *In Search of Lost Time* in which a madeleine dipped into a cup of tea transports the narrator back in time. Often, the foods we enjoyed as children have a special place in our adult affections, evoking pleasurable emotions.

In many countries, the production of food has become increasingly industrialized and technically complex. In 2014, in an attempt to raise cooking standards in restaurants, the French government introduced the label *fait maison*, to be used by restaurants to demonstrate that the food they serve has been made on the premises and not bought in, ready-prepared. The term 'ultra-processed food' is used to describe foods that contain additives and ingredients (emulsifiers, preservatives, sweeteners) not used in home kitchens. Recent research into such foods has linked their consumption to increased risks of cardiovascular and cerebrovascular disease. In response to health concerns, including over obesity, people's capacity to make meals 'from scratch' – that is, from basic ingredients – is regarded as a key foundation to a healthy lifestyle. Home cooking, for centuries a basic life skill, continues to be important.

Left, top: The Japanese artist Utagawa Kunisada was well known for his *ukiyo-e*, colourful woodblock prints depicting scenes from everyday life. Here he captures a tender, domestic scene – a seated woman peeling fruit while an eager-looking baby clambers on her shoulder.

Utagawa Kunisada (Toyokuni III), *The Cloth-fulling Jewel River*, 1830–45. Japan. Colour woodblock print on paper. H. 37.8 cm, W. 25.6 cm. 1906,1220,0.1083.

Left, bottom: There is a charming, domestic intimacy to the scene on this New Year's card, created by the French artist Jean Émile Laboureur. It depicts the artist and his family in their home, seated at their dining table, offering a toast.

Jean Émile Laboureur, *L'Artiste et sa famille (carte pour 1926)* (The artist and his family (card for 1926)), 1925. French. Etching and engraving on paper. H. 11.5 cm, W. 9.4 cm. 1949,0411.3040. Bequeathed by Campbell Dodgson.

Above: The starving Frenchman contrasted with a well-fed Englishman was a familiar subject for the eighteenth-century British caricaturist James Gillray. Here, a skeletal, barefoot revolutionary eating raw onions is countered by a grossly fat Englishman carving a large joint of raw beef.

James Gillray, *French Liberty. British Slavery*, 1792. Published in London, UK. Hand-coloured etching on paper. H. 25 cm, W. 35 cm. 1868,0808.6253.

Left: The artist Pierre Bonnard created his late still lifes while living and working in his home, Villa du Bosquet, in the south of France. His subjects were often household scenes, such as this simple meal on a table, characteristically portrayed using vivid colours.

Pierre Bonnard, *La Salle à manger, Villa du Bosquet, Le Carnet, France* (The Dining Room, Villa du Bosquet, Le Carnet, France), c. 1940. France. Graphite, watercolour and body colour on paper. H. 46.6 cm, W. 49 cm. 1981,0221.1.

HOSPITALITY

The sharing of food is at the heart of the concept of hospitality. The generosity demonstrated by the host in offering food and the mutual trust displayed by both the host and the guest in eating together is profound, especially when the guest is a stranger.

The idea of hospitality has long been central to many societies around the world; eating or drinking together is an important first step in creating and cementing social relationships. The word 'companion' comes from the Latin words *com*, meaning 'with', and *panis*, meaning 'bread' – so someone you break bread with. According to inviolate Bedouin traditions, once strangers visiting Bedouin camps had drunk the coffee their hosts had prepared for them, they were granted coffee and protection for a period of time – usually three days – to allow them to rest before resuming their journeys. In ancient Greece, the duties of hospitable obligation were passed down through the generations. Once a person had entertained a guest in their home, the descendants of both individuals were united by special bonds of 'guest-friendship' – bonds that were so powerful they could refuse to fight one another on the battlefield. In Christian monasteries, hospitality was regarded as a religious duty, with people who visited the monks given food and accommodation.

To be betrayed by one's host is a particular form of treachery. In *The Odyssey*, the ancient Greek epic poem attributed to Homer, Circe the sorceress invites Odysseus and his crew to feast with her in her home – and then

In Vanuatu, a savoury baked dish known as laplap is eaten on special occasions, shared among those present. In northern Vanuatu, men achieve status through a complex ceremonial cycle, and earn the right to own special objects, such as knives to cut the laplap. This knife would have belonged to a man of high status.

Ceremonial knife, before 1939. Ureparapara Island, Vanuatu. Wood. H. 46.9 cm, W. 9 cm, D. 7 cm. Oc1944,02.1066. Donated by Irene Marguerite Beasley.

The legend of Philemon and Baucis is told in Ovid's *Metamorphoses*. The gods Jupiter and Mercury disguise themselves as travellers seeking shelter for the night. They are repeatedly turned away by the town's wealthy households, but Philemon and Baucis take them into their lowly cottage.

Nicolaas Lauwers, Jupiter and Mercury in the home of Philemon and Baucis, c. 1630. The Netherlands. Engraving on paper. H. 48.4 cm, W. 55.4 cm. R,2.79. Bequeathed by Clayton Mordaunt Cracherode.

transforms them into swine. Only Odysseus, forewarned by the god Hermes and protected by the magic plant moly, is spared this fate. In Christianity, part of the resonance of the Last Supper lies in the fact that Judas Iscariot was prepared to betray Jesus even as he sat and ate bread with him. The risk of being poisoned saw rulers and aristocrats employ tasters to ensure that the food they were given was safe to eat. Similarly, dishes and drinking vessels were made from materials, such as jade, thought to possess special properties to protect against poison.

To this day, the act of hospitality brings with it certain codes of conduct. Generosity is often seen as a central requirement of true hospitality. Historically, this might have involved the killing of valuable livestock to honour the guest or the serving of precious foodstuffs. Hosts are judged by the generosity they show to their guests; in many cultures, the idea of not offering abundant food and drink is considered shameful. The guest should be looked after well and given the best of what's on the table, even if that means that the host and his or her family go without. With hospitality, one also finds the idea of reciprocation: the returning of one hospitable gesture with another. Someone who has been invited to a dinner party, for example, is expected, in turn, to invite the host to their own home for food and drink. At such events as dinner parties, social norms dictate that everyone present should make polite displays of consideration towards their fellow diners, like passing food or ensuring that drinks glasses are topped up.

In the world of work, the term 'hospitality industry' is used to describe a broad range of professional activities, including catering. As the term implies, in this industry – whether the business is an informal coffee shop or a luxurious restaurant – the notion that it should offer good, welcoming service remains integral. The ancient values implicit in the idea of hospitality continue to shape our social interactions to this day.

In this carving, the Yoruba wood carver Thomas Ona Odulate represents a European dinner party. Four figures are seated around a circular table, while cowrie shells and beads in a bowl in the centre represent food. Ondulate was noted for his sculptures depicting colonial life with a humorous twist.

Figure group, early 20th century. Made by Thomas Ona Odulate, Yoruba, Nigeria. Wood, cowrie shell. H. 17.8 cm, W. 15.9 cm, D. 16.4 cm. Af1954,23.142. Donated by Wellcome Institute for the History of Medicine.

Left: The drive to automate the production, sale and serving of food to reduce costs, such as wages, is an ongoing one. Cartoonist and illustrator William Heath Robinson was known for his humorous, satirical drawings of elaborate labour-saving devices, as in this dining-room scene.

William Heath Robinson, *How to Dispense with Servants in the Dining Room*, 1921. UK. Pen and black ink and watercolour on paper. H. 41.8 cm, W. 32.2 cm. 1967,1014.140. Bequeathed by Eric Millar.

Below: Victorian Britain saw a substantial increase in the number of middle-class households. These households employed servants to cook, serve, clean and look after their children for them. By 1900, 40.5 per cent of the adult female working population were in domestic service.

George du Maurier, *Circumstances after cases*, 1884. UK/France. Pen and brown ink on paper. H. 16.7 cm, W. 25.8 cm. 1967,1014.110. Bequeathed by Eric Millar.

FOOD SHOPPING

Food has been shared, bartered and sold for countless generations. The fact that we need to eat regularly and often means that access to foodstuffs is of great importance. For this reason, places that sell food have long played a key role in our villages, towns and cities. Prior to the widespread use of refrigeration, a pattern of daily shopping for fresh food was normal.

For centuries, food markets – at which the people who produced food could sell it to the people who needed it – were the principal places where food could be bought. As cities grew and developed, ensuring the supply of food to their populations so as to maintain civic order was an important matter for the authorities. In medieval Europe, the selling of food in cities took place on the streets, enabling the authorities to keep an eye on what was happening. Markets were held in public squares, with traders bringing in their wares and setting up temporary stalls, which were then packed up and taken away again – a means of trading that exists to this day. By their nature, food markets are important public spaces; indeed, market squares were often used for ceremonial public events. Busy marketplaces, thronging with people, were also used by orators, who found a ready audience for their rhetoric. Both the Agora of Athens and ancient Rome's Forum – important spaces for public assemblies – had their origins in food markets.

For reasons of convenience, market traders were often grouped together by the type of food they sold; this was the arrangement at the Agora in Athens. Over the centuries, as food shops started to open alongside traditional food

To this day, France remains a country noted for the quality and variety of its pastries, from eclairs to religieuse. Patisseries are a popular choice for those wishing to buy an edible gift as a dinner guest or a dessert to serve as a host.

Jean Émile Laboureur, *La Pâtisserie* (The Pastry Shop), 1914. France. Etching on paper. H. 18.6 cm, W. 20.4 cm. 1949,0411.2994. Bequeathed by Campbell Dodgson.

This early morning scene captures the hard work involved in transporting goods to food markets, something that remains true to this day. Two of the figures can be seen carrying fresh fish – a highly perishable foodstuff that, in pre-refrigeration days, had to reach potential buyers promptly.

Keisai Eisen, *First in the Series: Snowy Dawn at Nihonbashi*, c. 1835–42. Japan. Colour woodblock print on paper. H. 24.1 cm, W. 37 cm. 1906,1220,0.957.

markets, this specialization was maintained: bakers selling bread, butchers selling fresh meat, fishmongers offering seafood, greengrocers selling fresh fruit and vegetables. In Europe, grocers sold a range of processed and preserved foods: sugar, tea, coffee, spices and flour. Food shops of this type became a familiar sight on high streets. Cities saw the development of wholesale food markets, selling ingredients to smaller food retailers.

The twentieth century saw the rise of the supermarket, a type of food shop that traces its origins back to the grocery store. Whereas for centuries food shops had traditionally offered counter service to their customers, at the heart of the supermarket is the idea of self-service. An American grocer named Clarence Saunders played a significant role in the development of this form of food retail. In 1916, Saunders opened the Piggly Wiggly store in Memphis, Tennessee, where customers picked up a basket and filled it with groceries for themselves – a form of shopping we are familiar with today. While supermarkets have become popular in many countries, traditional food markets, held either outdoors or in purpose-built market halls, still exist. Since the 1970s, in such countries as the United States and Britain, there has been a renewed interest in farmers' markets, which seek to re-establish a direct connection between consumers and small-scale food producers.

Above: Inhabitants of the Roman auxiliary military fort of Vindolanda, close to Hadrian's Wall in the north of England, had to order their food in. Written in Latin on this wooden writing tablet is a shopping list for beans, chickens, apples, eggs, olives and fish sauce. The quantities suggest that the food was intended for several people, perhaps in the soldiers' mess.

Writing tablet, late 1st – early 2nd century CE. Vindolanda, UK. Wood. H. 4 cm, W. 10.7 cm. 1989,0602.17.

Left: The arrangement of foodstuffs in a manner intended to catch the eye of a potential customer remains an important aspect of food retail. Here, a man sits at a stall with his scales in hand, ready to serve. The colourful display of fresh produce includes grapes, peaches and the citrus fruit known as the Buddha's hand fruit.

Painting, late 18th century. Guangzhou, China. Ink and colour on paper. H. 42 cm, W. 30 cm. 1973,0918,0.1.1-158

Opposite: Traditionally, shopping for food involved being served individually by the staff working in the shop. The twentieth century, however, saw the rise of self-service food shopping – an idea pioneered in the United States – from which today's supermarkets are derived.

Mrs Munn, No. 53 *Fleet Market*, and *Aaron & John Trim, the Polite Grocers of No. 449 in the Strand*, 1808. Published in London, UK. Etching on paper. H. 20.3 cm, W. 12.1 cm. Heal,Portraits.194. Bequeathed by Sir Ambrose Heal.

Mrs. MUNN, No. 53, Fleet Market.

AARON & JOHN TRIM,
The Polite Grocers, of
No. 449, in the Strand

Freshness in meat is highly prized in Chinese cuisine, with most meat at Chinese markets sold on the day of slaughter – as depicted on this dish. In China, animal-derived foodstuffs like meat are deemed naturally to have an 'off' taste, which Chinese cooks, through techniques that include blanching and marinating, seek to remedy.

Dish, 1662–1722. Jingdezhen, China. Porcelain, enamel. H. 5.3 cm, Diam. 36.7 cm. Franks.405.b. Donated by Sir Augustus Wollaston Franks.

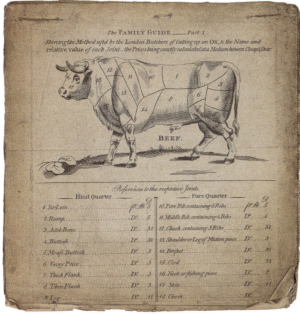

Left, top: As in many countries, meat in Britain was historically a luxury, not an everyday necessity like bread. In 1795, however, the price of the latter soared owing to a bad harvest the year before. In this satirical print, the politician William Pitt is portrayed as an arrogant butcher, thrusting a joint towards the impoverished figure of John Bull as a clearly unaffordable alternative to bread.

James Gillray, *The British butcher, supplying John Bull with a substitute for bread, vide message to Lord Mayor*, 1795. Published in London, UK. Hand-coloured etching on paper. H. 38.2 cm, W. 24.4 cm. 1868,0808.6455.

Left, bottom: The ability to carve up animal carcasses is central to the butcher's trade. When it comes to beef cattle, some cuts of meat, such as sirloin, are highly prized and priced accordingly, while others, such as shin, are sold more cheaply.

The Family Guide, early 19th century. UK. Engraving on paper. H. 20.7 cm, W. 18.5 cm. 1993,0620.22.1-12.

EATING UTENSILS

In some cultures, particular implements have been developed with which to prepare, serve and eat our food. One of the most fundamental of these is the knife. Given our blunt teeth, the need for a sharp blade of some kind, to cut such food as meat, has long been important. The first metal knives were fashioned from bronze during the early part of the first millennium BCE. In medieval and Renaissance Europe, people were expected to carry their own personal knife, which they used both as an eating utensil and, if need be, as a weapon. Courtly households employed specialist carvers to carve roast meat for their aristocratic employers. Over the centuries, a distinction developed between the sharp knives used in the kitchen for preparing food and the blunt table knives generally used for eating. As a result, special steak knives are brought out when the meat being served requires cutting with a sharper blade than those on table knives. Today, a great variety of culinary knives are available, usually made from stainless steel. Many are designed specifically for cutting just one type of food, such as bread, butter, cake, grapefruit, cheese or fish.

Spoons are another utensil with a long history. It is thought that the earliest spoons, used for eating liquid dishes like soups and stews, were made by tying shells onto sticks; the Latin word for 'spoon' comes from the word for 'shell'. Forks, however, are a far more recent addition to our tableware. While kitchen forks have a long history, it was the Italians who first adopted the fork as an eating tool in Europe, with seventeenth-century travellers to Italy commenting on this unusual dining habit. The novel implement nevertheless became fashionable, and by 1700 forks were in widespread use in Europe.

For centuries, wealthy people in Europe brought their own sets of knives to the table. This set, which consists of two large and two small knives with iron blades and handles decorated with silver gilt and enamel, was made in the early fifteenth century for John the Intrepid, Duke of Burgundy.

Group of knives and case, 1406 (knives), c. 1406–10 (case). France. Leather, wood, silver, enamel, iron. L. 38.8 cm (max), L. 40.2 cm (case). 1855,1201.118.

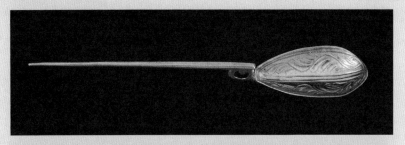

Decorated with leaves, this is one of eight spoons from a remarkable collection of Roman British tableware found near Mildenhall in Suffolk. Its shallow bowl and long stem suggest it might have been used for making a libation, a liquid offering to a deity.

Spoon, 4th century CE. West Row, UK. Silver. L. 17.1 cm. 1946,1007.34.

This ivory chopstick case, made in China in the last century of Manchu rule, holds a knife, a pair of chopsticks, a pick and some ear cleaners. Incised into the ivory is the story of a famous general of the Warring States period (481–221 BCE).

Chopstick case, 1800–1900. China. Ivory, silver, gold, brass. H. 29.4 cm, W. 2.5 cm, D. 2 cm. As1900,1119.8.a. Bequeathed by Henry Spencer Ashbee.

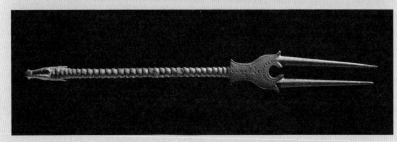

Dating to the late Sasanian period, this two-pronged bronze fork was excavated at Nineveh, modern-day Iraq, in 1874. Similar forks made of bronze or silver are known to have come from southern Iraq, Iran or Central Asia, and it seems that such items were in fashion for a while across the Sasanian empire.

Fork, 6th–7th century. Nineveh, Iraq. Copper alloy. L. 20.2 cm, W. 2.4 cm. SM.2489.

In China, Japan and Korea, chopsticks are used as eating implements. These slender objects originated in China; bronze chopsticks dating back to around 1200 BCE have been found in the ruins of Yin Xu, the last capital of the Shang dynasty, located close to modern-day Anyang City. Chopsticks have been fashioned from a range of materials: jade, ivory and lacquer for the wealthy, wood and bamboo for the poor. They are used for picking up small pieces of food, with the work of cutting done in the kitchen by the cook, rather than at the table by the diners. For this kitchen task, the Chinese have a special cleaver, which can be used in a variety of ways. One of the essential skills for a Chinese cook is the capacity to cut ingredients meticulously, whether slicing meat finely across the grain, cross-hatching squid, or chopping ginger into slender threads.

Left, top: Made as a gift, this dish was presented to the Tokugawa shogunate, the military government of Edo-period Japan, by the Nabeshima clan, rulers of Saga Domain (now Saga Prefecture). The design references two elements of Chinese mythology: the story of the hare in the moon, and, in its shape, the peaches of immortality.

Dish, 1700–50. Okawachi-yama, Japan. Porcelain. Diam. 14.5 cm. Franks.1292.+. Donated by Sir Augustus Wollaston Franks.

Left, bottom: Huge quantities of these so-called bevelled-rim bowls have been found at sites across the Middle East, from Syria to Iran. Dating to the fourth millennium BCE, they are the mass-produced equivalent of today's fast-food packaging, possibly discarded as soon as they were used.

Bowl, 3500–3000 BCE. Abu Shahrain (Eridu), Iraq. Pottery. H. 9.5 cm, Diam. 20.6 cm. 1919,1011.4620.

A roasted boar's head was often a centrepiece of the medieval feast table. This eye-catching eighteenth-century porcelain lidded bowl or tureen, made at the Chelsea factory for serving soup at the table, pays tribute to that tradition. It is modelled on the head of a hunted wild boar, with blood running from its mouth, eyes and ears.

Tureen, c. 1755. London, UK. Porcelain, enamel. H. 25.4 cm. 1940,0401.4. Bequeathed by Arthur Hurst.

This striking Qing-dynasty *famille rose* soup tureen takes the form of a naturalistically represented goose. It was designed to be used at the table, with the lid helping to keep the soup hot. Similar tureens were made in the shape of other birds and animals – including, as shown above, boars' heads.

Tureen, c. 1760–80. China. Porcelain. H. 33.5 cm, W. 23.6 cm, D. 37 cm. 1931,0622.8. Donated by Miss Ellen Carter.

GOOD NEWS

FOR ALL

HER MAJESTY'S LIEGE SUBJECTS

WHO WISH A GOOD

Breakfast, Dinner, Tea or Supper.

AT

37, MUSEUM STREET

(Two Doors from Great Russell Street)

THEY CAN HAVE

A DINNER FIT FOR A PRINCE

AT THE

MOST MODERATE CHARGES.

TEA, COFFEE OR COCOA,

Of the finest Quality and rarest Flavour.

PARTIES VISITING THE

ROYAL BRITISH MUSEUM

Are particularly requested to give this House of Refreshment a Trial, where they can be accommodated with all things requisite for making their Visit a pleasant one.

PRIVATE ROOMS FOR PARTIES.

All the Daily and Weekly Papers, Periodicals, Magazines, &c. being Food for the Mind, are liberally provided.

CHOPS, STEAKS, &c. done in a few Minutes.

Coffee made in the French Style, of the very best Mocha, at 2d. per Cup.

Eating out

Eating out, whether through necessity or for pleasure, has been a human pastime for thousands of years. With the biological need to eat has come the opportunity to satisfy that need by selling food and drink. In medieval Europe, such travellers as pilgrims or merchants were offered food and shelter by inns and taverns. Traders moving along the Silk Road were catered for at frequent intervals by caravanserais: roadside inns where they could rest and feed both themselves and their animals. Monasteries on pilgrimage routes offered hospitality in the form of food and accommodation. The history of restaurants is linked to large, prosperous cities that were centres of trade: Kaifeng, Hangzhou and Paris.

While restaurant franchises like McDonald's and Domino's are a twentieth-century phenomenon, there is a long history of people selling 'fast food' – cooked food ready to go. Excavations of the ancient Roman city of Pompeii, buried under ash in 79 CE, have revealed the presence of numerous *thermopolia*. These were Roman cookshops, selling cooked food to those who were too impoverished to possess their own kitchens; wealthy Romans, by contrast, possessed the space and servants to entertain their friends at home. In addition to cookshops, mobile street vendors selling snacks and drinks have traded for centuries, with the wares they offered an important source of food for the urban working classes. In *London Labour and the London Poor* (1851), the Victorian journalist Henry Mayhew lists pea soup, fried fish, meat puddings, assorted pies, sheep's trotters and hot eels as among the 'solids' that would comprise a meal.

The social aspect of dining out is also integral to its historic and ongoing popularity. Tea-houses, coffee-houses, chocolate-houses and cafes were places where people went not only to enjoy food and drink, but also for a chance to catch up with friends and exchange interesting news and gossip. Going out for food and drink in a public establishment brings with it the opportunity to meet people, network and make useful contacts. To this day, work meetings are often held over a meal or drink, whether a morning coffee, an after-hours beer or a lunch.

As they have done for hundreds of years, people also eat out purely for the pleasure of the food and the company. From a culinary point of view, restaurants offer a chance to try cuisines from different parts of the world, to sample the skills of a notable chef, or to eat dishes that one might struggle to make at home. The large range of eating-out experiences that are available to us today – from the informality of a picnic in a park with friends to a romantic meal with a loved one at a favourite restaurant – suggests that it will continue to be a popular pastime.

In 1815, the year in which Napoleon Bonaparte was defeated at the Battle of Waterloo, the French printmaker and satirist Philibert Louis Debucourt poked fun at boorish English eating manners with this print. The elegant waiter looks far more civilized than his English customer.

Philibert Louis Debucourt, *Gouter des Anglais* (English Taste), 1815. France. Hand-coloured aquatint, with stipple engraving on paper. H. 33 cm, W. 25.8 cm. 1861,1012.404. Donated by Henry W. Martin.

The historical antipathy between the two rival powers of England and France extended to their taste in food, which was a subject for satire in both nations. Here, a sturdy British sailor angrily rejects a plate of French food, demanding 'wholesome' fare, such as roast mutton.

Isaac Cruikshank (?), *An English Sailor at a French Eating House*, 1805. Published in London, UK. Hand-coloured etching with stipple on paper. H. 25.1 cm, W. 36 cm. 1948,0214.700.

Dealing with complaints is one of the duties of front-of-house staff in the hospitality industry. Here, in a historic variation of the 'Waiter, waiter, there's a fly in my soup' joke, an incredulous restaurant customer protests at being served a hatched egg.

Honoré Daumier, *Garçon, qu'est-ce que c'est que ça? …* (Waiter, what's this? …), 1841. Published in Paris, France. Lithograph, printed 'sur blanc' on paper. H. 19.9 cm, W. 20.2 cm. 1918,0511.230. Donated by Charles Rutherston.

Below, top: The Café des Mille Colonnes in Paris was noted for its gilt columns and for the stately elegance of its presiding lemonade-seller, Madame Romain. Here, she is sitting on a seat that once belonged to the Viceroy of Italy, attracting admiring glances.

Thomas Rowlandson, *La belle liminaudiere* [sic] *au caffee de Mille Collone. Palais Royal Paris* (The beautiful lemonade maker at the Mille Colonne café. Palais Royal Paris), 1814. Published in London, UK. Hand-coloured etching on paper. H. 17 cm, W. 24.9 cm.

Below, bottom: The small, informal eating establishments known as cafes had their origins in coffee houses; indeed, the word 'café' means 'coffee' in French. Such cafes as this Venetian example became fashionable spots in which to enjoy socializing and drinking.

Domenico Tiepolo, a cafe in Venice, *c.* 1800. Italy. Pen and brown ink, brown wash, over black chalk (some ruled), brown ink framing lines, on paper. H. 37.7 cm, W. 50.9 cm. 2011,7010.1. Donated by HM Government.

Opposite: Parisian cafes have long been popular meeting spots for France's artists, writers and thinkers. The Café de la Nouvelle Athènes, shown in this print, was frequented by the Impressionists, whose first exhibition was held in Paris in 1874. The cafe also appears in a painting by Degas.

Jean Louis Forain, *Le Café de la Nouvelle Athènes* (The New Athens Café), *c.* 1876. France. Etching with light surface tone, printed in brown ink on dull cream paper. H. 16.1 cm, W. 12.1 cm. 1949,0411.2725. Bequeathed by Campbell Dodgson.

COFFEE

For many people, the idea of getting through the day without a cup of coffee is unthinkable. Coffee's ability to stimulate our nervous systems – thanks to its caffeine content – is a key reason for its long popularity.

Coffee is made from the roasted, ground seeds (beans) of the coffee plant, with two varieties, *Coffea arabica* and *Coffea canephora* (from which robusta coffee derives), being the most commonly cultivated today. The origins of coffee lie in East Africa. *Coffea arabica*, the plant, is native to the highlands of this region, and, according to an Ethiopian legend, it was a goatherd who noticed the stimulating effects of the plant's berries after his flock had grazed on some of them. Coffee the drink, however, has its roots in Yemen during the late fourteenth or early fifteenth century, when it became popular among members of the Shadhiliyya Sufi religious order to prevent sleepiness and as an aid to mystic experiences. The coffee-drinking habit passed into secular life, spreading along the Arabian Peninsula to the Levant, and reaching Istanbul in the early 1500s. For centuries, Yemen had a monopoly on coffee cultivation. This ended in the early 1700s, when the Dutch managed to successfully cultivate coffee in their Southeast Asian colonies.

The dark, bitter brew was consumed in special drinking establishments known as coffee-houses. In the Islamic world, these were important secular meeting places where men could get together and converse over coffee. In Europe, the first coffee-houses were established in Livorno in 1632, Venice in 1640, Oxford in 1651 and London in 1652, with the exotic new drink initially regarded as a medicinal drug. Here, too, the social aspect of coffee-houses as meeting places was very important. During the seventeenth and eighteenth centuries, coffee-houses in Britain were nicknamed 'penny universities',

This coffee roaster (*mahmassa*), of a type used by Bedouins in the Levant, is shaped like a large spoon with a long handle and has wheels for easy removal from a floor-level fire. The coffee beans were then left to cool before being pounded or ground for brewing.

Roaster, 1920–70. Aleppo, Syria. Iron, brass. H. 28 cm, W. 22 cm, L. 78 cm. As1975,07.17.a.
Stirrer, 1920–70. Aleppo, Syria. Iron. L. 67 cm, W. 7 cm. As1975,07.17.b.

This watercolour painting depicts a *kahveci basi* (chief coffee-maker), whose principal task was to make coffee for the Ottoman sultan. They were also responsible for all the coffee-making equipment in the palace.

Painting, from *Costumes Turcs Vol. I*, c. 1790. Istanbul, Turkey. Watercolour on paper. H. 37.7 cm, W. 22 cm. 1974,0617,0.12.1.22.

as the price of a cup of coffee brought access to intellectual discussion and debate. The free exchange of ideas that took place in coffee-houses was often a cause of concern to the authorities, who feared subversion. There was also an economic dimension to this sharing of knowledge, with merchants, sailors and travellers visiting particular coffee-houses to share and gather news. Two major British financial institutions – the London Stock Exchange and the insurance brokers Lloyd's of London – have their origins in London coffee-houses, named Jonathan's and Lloyd's respectively.

The twentieth century saw a major innovation in the way coffee is brewed. In 1906, Luigi Bezzera and Desiderio Pavoni launched their Ideale coffee machine at the Milan International world's fair, using steam pressure to push water through finely ground coffee to create what Pavoni called *caffè espresso*. The espresso machine is at the heart of the many coffee shops found around the world today. These range from small, independent coffee shops and roasters, who pride themselves on the quality of their carefully crafted drinks, to large, international chains, offering a variety of coffee-based beverages.

Left: In the seventeenth century, London's street traders sold a diverse array of edible goods, from baked potatoes and meat pies to fresh fruit and ginger beer. Oysters, today regarded as a luxury in Britain, were a popular street food for centuries.

After Marcellus Laroon II, *Twelve Pence a Peck Oysters*, 1688. Published in London, UK. Etching on paper. H. 25 cm, W. 16.1 cm. L,85.23. Bequeathed by Sir Hans Sloane.

Below: Skewers of grilled meat and vegetables, traditionally cooked over charcoal, have long been popular in Japan. Here, a woman fans the charcoal while a man carries off a tray of *dengaku* – as the snacks are known – to sell to customers.

Sato Gyodai II, a man and woman prepare *dengaku*, 1876. Japan. Colour woodblock print on paper. H. 18.9 cm, W. 25.6 cm. 2021,3013.970. Purchase made possible by the JTI Japanese Acquisition Fund.

EATING OUT • STREET FOOD

Flatbreads have been a staple in Latin American cuisine for centuries, with many varieties tracing their origins to the pre-Columbian era. The nixtamalized corn tortilla remains a widely eaten food in Mexico. Here, a Day of the Dead skeleton tortilla-maker is shown producing her goods.

Figurine, 1980s. Mexico City, Mexico. Papier mâché, wood, paper. H. 30.5 cm, W. 16.5 cm, D. 19.5 cm. Am1989,12.23.

RESTAURANTS

Restaurants as we know them today – eating places with menus offering a variety of dishes and table service – took time to evolve. The first known restaurants appeared in China during the Song dynasty around 1100 CE. They opened in two extremely large cities, Kaifeng and Hangzhou, each with a population of more than 1 million and, importantly, each a major centre of trade. Merchants and bureaucrats were catered for by these restaurants, which specialized in regional cuisine and culinary styles and ranged from the casual to the formal. A memoir written in the early twelfth century by Meng Yuanlao includes a vivid description of a bustling Kaifeng restaurant where customers gave their orders to a waiter, who would then wait his turn in front of the kitchen before singing out his order to the cooks.

The story of the restaurant in Europe begins in eighteenth-century France. The French word *restaurant* initially meant a restorative broth. During the 1760s, Mathurin Roze de Chantoiseau opened a dining place in Paris serving *restaurants* (broths) to members of the public; in his *Almanach* of 1765, he calls himself a restaurateur offering 'exclusively those foods that either maintain or re-establish health'. From offering solely healthy broths, restaurants gradually changed, adding more dishes to their menus and seating diners at individual tables, rather than communal ones. Paris became home to a

Opposite: This woodblock print depicts a party at Shikian, a fashionable, exclusive restaurant on Nakazu, an artificial island in the Sumida River in Edo (Tokyo) that was later demolished. Among the food being served is a lucky *tai* fish (sea bream), while two geishas can be seen tuning their *shamisen*.

Kubo Shunman, a party at Shikian restaurant, c. 1787–88. Edo, Japan. Colour woodblock diptych print on paper. H. 36.3 cm, W. 25.3 cm (each sheet). 1924,0327,0.9.1-2. Donated by Robert N. Shaw.

Left: This Victorian advertisement for a restaurant on a street in front of the British Museum, which it wrongly calls the Royal British Museum, plays on patriotism to encourage customers to eat there. The same street still has many eating places, catering for the millions of visitors to the Museum.

Advertisement, c. 1850. Published in London, UK. Letterpress on paper. H. 18.7 cm, W. 12.3 cm. 1983,U.2345.

number of noticeably splendid restaurants. In 1782, La Grande Taverne de Londres opened in the Palais-Royal, commended by the gourmand Brillat-Savarin for its elegant setting, smart waiters, fine wines and excellent food. Along with the proliferation of restaurants in the city, there also came restaurant critics. In 1803, Alexandre-Balthazar-Laurent Grimod de La Reynière published *Almanach des Gourmands*, containing reviews of Parisian restaurants and advice on such matters as how to order food, in which order to eat dishes and how to use eating utensils correctly.

The French model of a grand, formal restaurant was an influential one. During the following centuries, however, restaurants continued to adapt, mirroring the social changes taking place around them. In the last decades of the nineteenth century, for example, more dining options became available for middle-class women. The twentieth century saw the rise of informal dining-out, with franchise restaurants like McDonald's offering a popular business model. Today, restaurants exist around the world in many forms. They range from standardized chains, offering affordable fast food in a casual setting, to luxurious restaurants owned by famous chefs, noted for the quality of their food and drink.

EATING OUT • PICNIC SCENES

Opposite: Picnicking was a popular subject in Mughal art, with picnic-related scenes including kings with their courtiers around them or lovers enjoying a romantic alfresco meal. Here, a woman sits in an elegant pavilion in a rural setting by a stream, her servants in attendance.

Painting, c. 1750. India. Paper. H. 30 cm, W. 20 cm. 1951,0407,0.21. Donated by Miss N. Campbell.

Above, top: In nineteenth-century Britain, picnicking outdoors became a popular pastime among the middle classes. Picnics offered a way of experiencing the charms of nature – the fresh air, the beauty of the rural landscape – in the company of friends and family.

Joseph Mallord William Turner, *Richmond Hill and Bridge, Surrey*, c. 1831. UK. Watercolour, touched with body colour on paper. H. 29.1 cm, W. 43.5 cm. 1958,0712.435. Bequeathed by Robert Wylie Lloyd.

Above: The delicate, transient beauty of *sakura* (cherry blossoms) has been appreciated in Japan for centuries. The traditional spring custom of *hanami* (blossom viewing) has developed, with groups of people gathering to enjoy food and drink together outdoors under cherry trees.

Utagawa Hiroshige, *An Excursion to Gotenyama*, 1840s–50s. Japan. Colour woodblock print on paper. H. 25.2 cm, W. 37.5 cm. 1906,1220,0.900.

Left, top: The bento box, Japan's portable food container, is said to trace its origins to the Momoyama period (1568–1600), when lacquered, wooden boxes were used to carry the single-portion meal known as a *bento*. This ingeniously constructed Edo-period example features several compartments and containers for heating water and storing food.

Pair of travelling boxes for food, 17th–19th century. Japan. Wood, lacquer, metal. H. 37.8 cm, W. 34.5 cm, D. 34.5 cm each. 1998,0610.1-2.

Left, bottom: This Mamluk-dynasty lunch box consists of a series of separate containers, originally held together by metal pins. The engraved decoration includes a repeated inscription in Arabic: 'He who contemplates my beauty will find me a delight to the eye. I have a form which includes all the essence of good.'

Lunch box, 15th–16th century. Egypt. Brass. H. 18.4 cm, Diam. 13 cm. 1908,0328.2.

Opposite: In this colourful sculpture, the artist Richard Glazer-Danay, who is of Caughnawaga Mohawk and Jewish descent, uses a lunchpail (a form of lunch box that originated in North America) to juxtapose an iconic American monument, the Statue of Liberty, with a bottle of beer, creating out of metal a homage to the significant role of the 'Mohawk Skywalkers'. These ironworkers helped construct many of the buildings that make up iconic North American skylines today.

Sculpture, c. 1983. Made by Richard Glazer-Danay, Mohawk, Haudenosaunee (Iroquois Confederacy), USA. H. 28.5 cm, W. 34 cm. Am1983,37.1. Donated by Richard Glazer-Danay.

Food and our future

Respect for food was woven into the fabric of hunter-gatherer societies around the world. For the Indigenous peoples of the Arctic, for example, it was important to use every part of a creature that had been caught and killed. The Inuit would carefully butcher a walrus carcass to extract every edible part, from the innards to the fat. The intestine was used to make waterproof coats, the liver membrane to make drums, and the tusks to make ivory tools and carvings.

Today, in contrast to this low-waste approach, it is estimated that nearly a third of the food produced by humans is wasted. This wastage occurs throughout the food chain. Crops are lost for a variety of reasons, among them pests, disease, inefficient irrigation and harvesting, and poor storage, which results in food spoilage. A sizeable percentage of food is simply thrown away, either by retailers or by households.

Food waste has environmental consequences. Food that is allowed to rot in landfill sites emits methane, a potent greenhouse gas that contributes towards global warming. Producing food also involves emissions, which, if the food is not eaten, are even more costly. Indeed, it is estimated that food waste is the cause of between 8 and 10 per cent of the Earth's total greenhouse-gas emissions. In the United States, a 2021 Environmental Protection Agency report showed that, in America, food is the most common material put into landfill or incinerated, making up more than a fifth of landfilled or combusted municipal solid waste. Food waste is an issue for societies around the world: household food waste per capita is similar in high-, upper-middle- and lower-income countries.

In a world affected by climate change and in which millions of people go hungry, reducing food waste is an important goal. 'Sustainability' has become a buzzword in the world of food, although what this means exactly and how to achieve it is complex. An awareness that soil is a precious resource that needs preserving is leading farmers to explore regenerative farming systems, improving the health of their soil while reducing their chemical inputs. Influential chefs have embraced a 'nose to tail' approach to the food they offer in their restaurants, serving unfashionable cuts and offal to diners who have become unfamiliar with them.

Our own households, too, can play their part in tackling food waste. Simple steps, like making meal plans, buying only the food we need and using up or composting any leftovers rather than throwing them in the bin, can help reduce wastage. Indeed, dishes that make use of such leftovers as stale bread, cooked rice, boiled potatoes and roast-chicken carcasses can be found in many cuisines. What was once termed 'good housekeeping' – embracing thriftiness rather than extravagance and the ability to conjure up a family meal from a few ingredients – has long been seen as an admirable skill. In the battle against food waste, reconnecting with the idea that food is simply too precious to waste seems like a good place to start.

Bibliography

Akbarnia, Ladan, *et al.*, *The Islamic World: A History in Objects* (London: Thames & Hudson in collaboration with the British Museum, 2018)

Black, Maggie, *The Medieval Cookbook*, rev. edn (London: The British Museum Press, 2012)

Bolton, Lissant, *Baskets and Belonging: Indigenous Australian Histories* (London: The British Museum Press, 2011)

Caygill, Marjorie, *Treasures of the British Museum* (London: The British Museum Press, 2009)

Christian, David, *This Fleeting World: A Short History of Humanity* (Great Barrington, MA: Berkshire Publishing Group, 2015)

Coe, Sophie D., and Coe, Michael D., *The True History of Chocolate* (London: Thames & Hudson, 1996)

Crane, Eva, *The World History of Beekeeping and Honey Hunting* (London: Routledge, 1999)

Crosby, Alfred W., Jr, *The Columbian Exchange: Biological and Cultural Consequences of 1492* (Westport, CT: Praeger, 2003)

Dalby, Andrew, and Grainger, Sally, *The Classical Cookbook*, rev. edn (London: The British Museum Press, 2012)

Davidson, Alan, *The Oxford Companion to Food* (Oxford: Oxford University Press, 1999)

Diamond, Jared, *Guns, Germs and Steel: A Short History of Everybody for the Last 13,000 Years* (London: Vintage, 1998)

d'Offay, Timothy, *Easy Leaf Tea: Tea House Recipes to Make at Home* (London: Ryland Peters & Small, 2017)

Donnelly, Catherine (ed.), *The Oxford Companion to Cheese* (Oxford: Oxford University Press, 2016)

Dunlop, Fuchsia, *Invitation to a Banquet: The Story of Chinese Food* (London: Particular Books, 2023)

Ellis, Hattie, *Sweetness and Light: The Mysterious History of the Honey Bee* (London: Sceptre, 2004)

Fernández-Armesto, Felipe, *Food: A History* (London: Macmillan, 2001)

Freeman, Michael, and d'Offay, Timothy, *The Life of Tea: A Journey to the World's Finest Teas* (London: Mitchell Beazley, 2018)

Graeber, David, and Wengrow, David, *The Dawn of Everything: A New History of Humanity* (London: Penguin, 2021)

Green, Alexandra, *Southeast Asia: A History in Objects* (London: Thames & Hudson in collaboration with the British Museum, 2023)

Harari, Yuval Noah, *Sapiens: A Brief History of Humankind* (London: Vintage, 2011)

Harrison-Hall, Jessica, *China: A History in Objects* (London: Thames & Hudson in collaboration with the British Museum, 2017)

Hooper, Steven, *Pacific Encounters: Art and Divinity in Polynesia 1760–1860* (London: The British Museum Press, 2006)

Kiple, Kenneth, and Ornelas, Kriemhild Coneè (eds), *The Cambridge World History of Food* (Cambridge: Cambridge University Press, 2000)

Kurlansky, Mark, *Cod: A Biography of the Fish that Changed the World* (London: Vintage, 1999)

Laudan, Rachel, *Cuisine and Empire: Cooking in World History* (Berkeley, CA: University of California Press, 2013)

Lincoln, Amber, Cooper, Jago, and Loovers, Jan Peter Laurens (eds), *Arctic: Culture and Climate* (London: Thames & Hudson in collaboration with the British Museum, 2020)

Linford, Jenny, *The Seven Culinary Wonders of the World: A History of Honey, Salt, Chile, Pork, Rice, Cacao, and Tomato* (Washington, DC: Smithsonian Books, 2018)

McGee, Harold, *McGee on Food and Cooking: An Encyclopedia of Kitchen Science, History and Culture* (London: Hodder & Stoughton, 2004)

MacGregor, Neil, *A History of the World in 100 Objects* (London: Allen Lane, 2010)

Mair, Victor H., and Hoh, Erling, *The True History of Tea* (London: Thames & Hudson, 2009)

Marzinzik, Sonja, *Masterpieces: Early Medieval Art* (London: The British Museum Press, 2013)

Owen, Sri, *The Rice Book: The Definitive Book on the Magic of Rice Cookery* (London: Doubleday, 1993)

Rawson, Katie, and Shore, Elliott, *Dining Out: A Global History of Restaurants* (London: Reaktion Books, 2019)

Saladino, Dan, *Eating to Extinction: The World's Rarest Foods and Why We Need to Save Them* (London: Jonathan Cape, 2021)

Sen, Colleen Taylor, *Feasts and Fasts: A History of Food in India* (London: Reaktion Books, 2015)

Simpson, St John, 'The Royal Table', in J. Curtis and N. Tallis (eds), *Forgotten Empire: The World of Ancient Persia* (London: The British Museum Press, 2005), pp. 104–11

Spencer, A. J. (ed.), *The British Museum Book of Ancient Egypt*, rev edn (London: The British Museum Press, 2007)

Standage, Tom, *An Edible History of Humanity* (London: Atlantic Books, 2010)

Steel, Carolyn, *Hungry City: How Food Shapes Our Lives* (London: Vintage, 2009)

Tannahill, Reay, *Food in History*, rev. edn (London: Penguin, 1988)

Visser, Margaret, *Much Depends on Dinner: The Extraordinary History and Mythology, Allure and Obessions, Perils and Taboos of an Ordinary Meal* (London: Penguin, 1986)

Wilson, Bee, *Consider the Fork: A History of Invention in the Kitchen* (London: Particular Books, 2012)

Wrangham, Richard, *Catching Fire: How Cooking Made Us Human* (London: Profile Books, 2010)

Acknowledgments

All books are collective endeavours, especially a book of this nature. My thanks to Julian Honer of Thames & Hudson and Claudia Bloch of the British Museum for thinking of me for this fascinating project and for all their help and support.

At Thames & Hudson, my thanks, also, to Julie Hrischeva for her interest and input; Mark Ralph for his thoughtful, meticulous copy-editing; Peter Dawson (Grade Design) for his notable design skills; and Robert Heath, Production Controller.

At the British Museum, my thanks to Laura Meachem of the Publishing team for all her hard work.

I am very grateful to the British Museum staff, past and present, who kindly took the time and trouble to share their knowledge and expertise with me to help create this book: Julie Adams, Helen Anderson, Daniel Antoine, Georgia Barker, Rosina Buckland, Hugo Chapman, Alice Christophe, Jill Cook, Zoe Cormack, Irving Finkel, Alexandra Green, Alfred Haft, Emily Hannam, Jessica Harrison-Hall, Richard Hobbs, Tom Hockenhull, Julie Hudson, Sushma Jansari, Sang-ah Kim, Rachel King, Zeina Klink-Hoppe, Ruiliang Liu, Yu-Ping Luk, Shiva Mihan, Beverley Nenk, Thorsten Opper, Jane Portal, Imma Ramos, Ilona Regulski, Sandra Sattler, St John Simpson, Julia Stribblehill, Jonathan Taylor, Rose Taylor, Awet Teklehimanot Araya, Marie Vandenbeusch, Alexandra Villing, Mei Xin Wang, Akiko Yano and Danny Zborover.

My thanks, too, to the British Museum photography team – Joanna Fernandes, Stephen Dodd, David Agar, Marco Borsato, Bradley Timms and Isabel Marshall – for their work photographing these remarkable objects and to the curators and collection managers for their help with this process.

Finally, I am grateful to Tim d'Offay and Rachael Sills for kindly sharing their tea and cheese knowledge; much appreciated.

Picture credits

The publisher would like to thank the copyright holders for granting permission to reproduce the images illustrated. Every attempt has been made to trace accurate ownership of copyrighted images in this book. Any errors or omissions will be corrected in subsequent editions provided notification is sent to the publisher. Further information about the Museum and its collection can be found at britishmuseum.org. Registration numbers for British Museum objects are included in the image captions. All images of British Museum objects are © 2025 The Trustees of the British Museum, courtesy the Department of Photography and Imaging.

Page 10: reproduced by permission of the artist; page 16: © the artist; page 54 (bottom): reproduced by permission of the artist; page 55: reproduced by permission of the artist's estate; page 75 (bottom): reproduced by permission of the artist's estate; page 86: photo courtesy of David Coulson, TARA; page 191: reproduced by permission of the artist's estate; page 247: reproduced by permission of the artist's estate.

Index

Note: page numbers in *italic* refer to the illustrations.

agriculture
    animals 85–105
    plants 63–83
alcohol 153–71
    see also beer; wine
Algeria 86
American War of Independence 70
animals
    agriculture 85–105
    animal sacrifice 89, *96*, *102*, 123, *124–5*
    dairy products 85, 88–9, 92, 93, 180–2, *180–3*
    domestication 85, 88, 92, 98, 102
    draught animals 85, 92, *104–5*
    hunting 13–27
aquaculture 45, 51
Arctic *see* Inuit
Assyria *46*, *97*, 137, *139*
Australia *14*, *24*, 30, *32*
Austria *159*

bakers 205, *205*, 223
Bali 34, *67*
Bangladesh *9*
banquets *see* feasts
baskets 29, *30–1*, *40*, *203*
Bedouins 218, *238*
beer 153, *154–7*, *156–7*, *162–3*, 204–5
bees *see* honey
birds, hunting for *20–1*, *22–3*
boar, wild *18–19*, 102
boats and ships
    fishing boats 45, *47–8*, *52–3*
    Inuit hunting 17
    overseas trade *109*, *113*, *120–1*
    table ornament *149*
Borneo *31*, *78*
bread 71, 204–5, *204–5*
Buddhism *80*, 123, *127*, *132–3*, *143*, 153, *190–1*, *224*
Burma *117*, *127*
butchers 223, *226–7*

cacao *see* chocolate
cafes 233, *236–7*
Cambodia *105*
camels 85, *112*
Cameroon *30*, *40*, *188*, *196*
Canada *15*, *31–2*, *56*, 57
    see also Inuit
cattle 85, *86*, 92–3, *92–5*
cereals 63, 70–1, 76–7
    see also rice; wheat
cheese 88–9, 173, *174*, 181, *182*
chickens 98, *99–101*
chilli 107, 114, *119*, *175*
chilling 34, *164–5*
China
    agriculture 66, *66*, 80, *80*, 81, *82*, *100*, 102, *103*, *104–5*
    banquets 137
    chopsticks 229, *229*
    food shopping *224*
    hunting 23, 27
    porcelain *66*, *82*, *100*, *113*, *120*, *159*, *169–70*, *179*, *190*, *193*, *226*, *231*
    prints *80*, *104*, *209–10*
    religion 123, *127–8*, *128–9*, *133*
    restaurants 242
    rice wine 166–7, *169*
    salt 176
    soup 198, *199*
    tea 190–1, *190*, *192–3*
chocolate 114–15, *114–15*
chopsticks 229, *229*
Christianity 134–5, *145*, 161, 219
    Easter 123, *134*, 142
    fasting 45, 56, 142, *142*
    symbolism 89, *90*, 204
    see also monasteries
citrus 80–1
climate change 16, 63, 248–9
cod 56–7

coffee and coffee-houses 218, 233, *236*, 238–9, *238–9*
Columbian Exchange 107
Columbus, Christopher 77, 80, 102, 107, 114
condiments 173, *178–9*
    see also salt
Cook Islands *48*
cooking 23, 51, 57, 98, 195–213
cooks *206–7*
corn *see* maize
cutlery *see* eating utensils

dairy products 85, 88–9, 92, 93, 180–2, *180–3*
dogs 13, *19–20*, 23–4, *207*
domestication of animals 85, 88, 92, 98, 102
draught animals 85, 92, *104–5*
drinking 34–5, 153–71
    vessels *150–1*, *158–9*
    see also beer; wine
drunkenness 153, *169–71*
ducks 99
Dutch *see* Netherlands

Easter 123, *134*, 142
eating in 215–31
eating out 233–46
eating utensils 228–9, *228–9*
eggs 98, *98*, 123, *134*
Egypt, ancient
    alcohol *155*, 156, *157*, 160
    beekeeping 40–1
    bread 204–5, *205*
    food for the dead 128, *129*, *157*
    papyrus *78–9*
    pottery and terracotta *155*, *208*
    religion 93, 123
    tomb-painting *20*
Egypt, Mamluk-dynasty lunch box *246*
England *see* United Kingdom
environmental issues 45, 85, 248–9
Ethiopia *65*, 71, *176*, *204*, 238
Etruscans *138*, *149*, 184

falconry *26–7*
farming *see* agriculture
fasting and abstinence 45, 56, 123, 142–3, *142–3*, 153, *170*
feasts 137–51
Fiji *11*
Finland *197*
fish and fishing 45–61
    see also shellfish
flour 71, 173, *189*, 204, *204–5*
food carriers *246–7*
food for the dead 128–9, *128–9*, *157*
food offerings 123, *126–7*
    animal sacrifice 89, *96*, *102*, 123, *124–5*
food waste 248–9
foraging 29, *36–7*, *39*
    see also hunter-gatherers
France
    Ice Age *6*, *14*, *61*
    ivories *27*
    metalwork *73*, *144*, *149*, *228*
    paintings, drawings and prints *79*, *99*, *116*, *130*, *178*, *206–7*, *216–17*, *222*, *234–7*
    restaurants and cafes *236–7*, *242–3*
fruit *42–3*, 80–1, *82–3*

game animals 13, *22–3*
gathering 29–43
geese *99*
Germany
    brewing beer *156*, 157
    metalwork *149*
    paintings, drawings and prints *49*, *58*, *81*, *135*, *145*, *189*
    stoneware *154*, *156*
    walrus ivory draughts piece *92*
Ghana *125*, *208*
goats 85, *96–7*
grain 63, 70–1, 76–7
    grinding into flour 173, *189*, 204, *205*
    see also beer; rice; wheat
Grand Exchange 107
Greece, ancient
    animal sacrifice 123, *124–5*
    coins *184*
    food shopping 222–3
    hospitality 218–19
    pottery *19*, *50*, *121*, *125*, *160*, *165*, *185*

    terracotta *174*
    wine 160, *160*, 161, *165*
Guatemala *115*
Guinea-Bissau *33*

Hinduism 93, *95*, 123, *126*, 137, 142, 143, *180*
home cooking 215
    see also eating in; kitchens
Honduras *76*
honey 40–1
horses 85
hospitality 218–19, *218–19*
hunter-gatherers 13, 29, 63
hunting 13–27

Incas *87*, 123, 156
India 80, *90*, *113*, 137, 143, *180*
    paintings and drawings *89*, *95*, *126*, *168*, *245*
    sugar 110, *111*
    tea *190*, 191
    see also Hinduism; Mughal Empire
Indonesia 34, *67*, *109*, *113*, 118–19
inns and taverns 153, *170*, 233
Inuit *16–17*, *16–17*, *55*, *60*, 248
Iran *112*, *120*, *140*
    see also Persia
Iraq *94*, *120*, *229*, *230*
    see also Assyria; Ur
Ireland *200*
Islam 89, 137, *140*, 204, 238
    fasting *131*, 142, 143
    forbidden foods and drinks 103, 123, 153
Italy
    drawings and prints *21*, *69*, *142*, *183*, *187*, *209*
    earthenware *18*, *164*
    see also Etruscans; Rome, ancient, and Roman Empire; Venice

Jainism 123, 153
Japan
    bento box *246*
    drawings and paintings *58–9*, *100*, *109*, *132*, *166*
    netsuke *43*, *155*, *187*, *193*
    pottery and porcelain *167*, *196*, *198*, *230*
    prints *19*, *37–8*, *46*, *51*, *65*, *141*, *170*, *203*, *213*, *216*, *223*, *240*, *242*, *245*

    rice wine (*sake*) *58*, *155*, *166–7*, *167*, *170*
    soup *198*, 199
Judaism 80, 103, 123, *130*, 142, 161, 199, 204

kitchens *206*, *209*, 210–11, *210–13*
Korea *127*, *144*, *175*, 229

lemons 80, 81
llamas *87*
London
    coffee-houses 238–9
    restaurants *243*
    street traders 233, *240*

maize 76–7
Malaysia *25*, *35*, 202
    see also Borneo
markets 222–3, *223*, *226*
Marshall Islands *108*
Maya 76, 77, 114, *115*
Mesoamerica
    chocolate 114, *115*
    maize 76, 77
    see also Guatemala; Honduras; Mexico
Mexico 76, 114, *114*, 129, *129*, *241*
milk *see* dairy products
Mixtec culture *114*
Moluccas *109*, 118–19
monasteries, Christian 45, 153, 156, 161, 218, 233
Morocco 81, *131*
Mughal empire 26, *158*, *168*, *244*
mushrooms 38–9
Muslims *see* Islam
mussels 37, 50–1, *212*
mustard *179*
Mycenaean civilization *50*

Netherlands
    delftware *179*
    Dutch traders and colonialists *113*, 119, 191, 238
    paintings, drawings and prints *23*, *37*, *52*, *83*, *201*, *213*, *219*
New Caledonia *68*
New Zealand *131*
Newfoundland *56*, *57*
Nigeria *186*, *220*
nixtamalization 77, *241*
nutmeg 118–19, *119*
nuts, gathering *42–3*

olive oil 179, 184–5, *184–5*
oranges 80, 81
oysters 33, 50, 51, *213*, *240*

Pakistan *117*, 143
Papua New Guinea 87, *174*
Paris, restaurants and cafes 236–7, 242–3
Persia 89, 96, 98, 146
Peru
    llama figurine *87*
    pottery 22, *47*, *119*, 154
    see also Incas
picnicking 140, 233, *244–5*
pigs and pork 85, *87*, 102–3, *102–3*, 123
plants, agriculture 63–83
Poland 134
Pompeii *205*, 233
pork see pigs and pork
Portugal 56, 57, 118–19, *186*, 191
potato 74, 107
poultry 98–9, *99–101*
preserving and processing 173–93

religion 123–35
    animal sacrifice 89, 96, 102, 123, *124–5*
    customs and traditions 130–1
    see also Buddhism; Christianity; fasting and abstinence; Hinduism; Islam
restaurants 215, 233, 234–5, 242–3, *242–3*
rice 65–8, *66–7*, *202*
rice wine
    China 166–7, *169*
    Japan (*sake*) 58, 155, 166–7, *167*, *170*
Rome, ancient, and Roman Empire
    agriculture 90, 99, 101–2, *104*
    beekeeping 41
    bread 205, *205*
    feasts 139, 147, 150
    fishing and seafood 50, *59*
    food shopping *224*, 233
    metalwork 90, *102*, *104*, 147, *197*, *229*
    olive oil 184
    pottery and terracotta *96*, *182*, *208*
    religion *96*, *102*, 123
    travel and trade 107
    wine 161
Russia *64*

saffron 119
sake see rice wine, Japan
salt 173, 176–7, *176–7*, 186
    salting fish 45, 57
sea and seashore, foraging 36–7
sheep 85, 88–9, *88–91*
shellfish 33, 37, 50–1, *212–13*, *240*
ships see boats and ships
shopping for food 222–3, *222–5*, 233
slave trade 107, *110*, 111
social drinking 162–3
Solomon Islands 52–3, *60*, 146
soup 198–9, *198–9*, 231
Spain
    prints *212*
    Spanish in the New World 66, 77, 80, 99, 107, 114
Spice Islands *109*, 118–19
spices 118–19, *118–19*
Straits Settlements *202*
street food 233, *240–1*
sugar 110–11, *110–11*, 173
supermarkets 223
Switzerland *182*
Syria 151, *238*

taboos 103, 123
Tanzania *25*
tea 190–1, *190–3*
Temperance movements 35, 153, *171*
trade see travel and trade
transport see boats and ships; draught animals
travel and trade 107–21
Turkey *101*, 148, *239*
turkeys 99

United Kingdom
    collage *42*
    drinking horns *162*
    glass *110*
    hunting horn *24*
    metalwork *104*, *108*, *115*, 118–19, *135*, *147–8*, *150–1*, *164*, *197*, *200*, *229*
    paintings and drawings *39*, *48*, *53*, *72*, *74–5*, *103*, *181*, *212*, *221*, *245*
    pottery and porcelain *91*, *163*, *182*, *231*
    prints *36*, *39*, *41*, *54*, *57*, *75*, *83*, *141*, *171*, *189*, *191*, *199*, *211*, *217*, *225*, *227*, *235–6*, *240*, *243*; woodcuts/wood engravings *21*, *43*, *88*, *94*, *207*
    wooden objects *8*, *224*
United States of America
    banknote from Pennsylvania *70*
    cowboys *93*
    Indigenous peoples *34*, *60*, 77, *203*, *246*
    see also Inuit
    Prohibition 153, *169*
Ur *82*, *162–3*

Vanuatu *218*
vegetables, growing 74–5
vegetarianism 123, 137
Venice *110*, 118, *142*, *161*, *177*, 236, 238
Vietnam *10*, *54*, 68
vinegar *132*, 173, *178–9*

water, human need for 34–5
weddings *114*, 137, 144–5, 167, *167*
weighing and weights 116–17, *125*, *208*
wheat 70–1, 107, 166, 204
wine 73, 153, *154*, 158–61, *160–1*, *163–5*, *168–9*
    feasting 137, 139–40, 145, *147–8*
    see also rice wine

Yemen *238*

For my mother, Lydia Linford, with love and gratitude

Frontispiece: Nicolaas Lauwers, Jupiter and Mercury in the home of Philemon and Baucis, c. 1630 (see page 219).

First published in the United Kingdom in 2025 by
Thames & Hudson Ltd, 181A High Holborn, London WC1V 7QX
in collaboration with the British Museum

First published in the United States of America in 2025 by
Thames & Hudson Inc., 500 Fifth Avenue, New York, New York 10110

Repast: The Story of Food © 2025 The Trustees of the British Museum/
Thames & Hudson Ltd, London

Text © 2025 The Trustees of the British Museum
Images © 2025 The Trustees of the British Museum
Design © 2025 Thames & Hudson Ltd, London

Designed by Peter Dawson, www.gradedesign.com

All images are of British Museum objects, courtesy the Department of Photography and Imaging, unless otherwise stated on page 252.

All Rights Reserved. No part of this publication may be reproduced or transmitted in any form or by any means, electronic or mechanical, including photocopy, recording or any other information storage and retrieval system, without prior permission in writing from the publisher.

British Library Cataloguing-in-Publication Data
A catalogue record for this book is available from the British Library

Library of Congress Control Number 2024951486

ISBN 978-0-500-48115-8

Impression 01

Printed and bound in China by C&C Offset Printing Co. Ltd

For more information about the Museum and its collection, please visit
britishmuseum.org.

Be the first to know about our new releases,
exclusive content and author events by visiting
thamesandhudson.com
thamesandhudsonusa.com
thamesandhudson.com.au